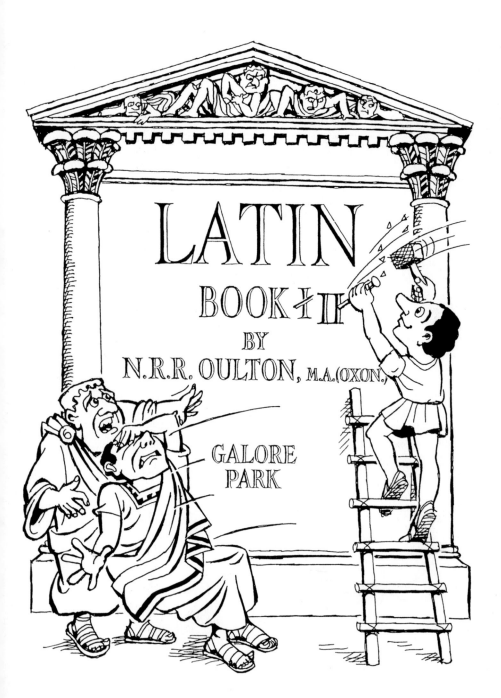

Hodder Education, an Hachette UK Company,
Carmelite House, 50 Victoria Embankment,
London EC4Y 0DZ

Typesetting by Typetechnique
Printed in India

ISBN-13: 978 1 902984 01 8

An answer book is available to accompany this book:

ISBN-13: 978 1 902984 06 3

First published 1999
Reprinted 2001, 2002, 2005, 2007, 2010, 2011, 2013, 2014, 2016

Details of other Galore Park publications are available at www.galorepark.co.uk
ISEB Revision Guides, publications and examination papers may also be obtained from Galore Park.

Contents

Acknowledgements

The author would like to thank the following who have all contributed to the production of this book:

Theo Zinn and Stephen Anderson, who read the proofs of the book and pointed out its numerous faults and errors with great tact and infinite patience – the errors that remain are, of course, entirely my own; the girls of Tormead School, who put up with the various revisions of the book and pointed out its faults and misprints on a daily basis; in particular I should like to thank Nikki Lake, who shot through the original version of the whole course in two terms flat and pointed out several glaring errors with an ever cheerful "It's probably me, but shouldn't there be a verb in this sentence...?"; Roland Smith, for coping with the endless stream of "last minute changes"; Honor Alleyne, for inspiring me to write the book in the first place, and for allowing me to inflict it on the girls of Tormead without so much as a government health warning; Elizabeth Bowder for the music setting of the Perfect Passive song; and the countless colleagues who have commented on this and earlier versions of the book and given me their support. I shall not give the traditional acknowledgement to my wife, Claire, because she said she would kill me if I did.

PREFACE

So, you made it through Book I and are on for more? Well, here we go again then. Things on the left have to be learnt. Things on the right have to be done. Vocab. has to be learnt both ways (*into* and *out of* Latin) and, most important of all, jokes have to be acknowledged with a short burst of uncontrollable laughter.

We assume that you are totally happy with everything covered in Book I: regular verbs in the six active tenses; nouns of the first three declensions; 1st/2nd declension adjectives; the use of prepositions. If you're not totally happy about any of the above, go back and learn it again! Remember, there are no short cuts. Just get your head down and learn it.

I said in the preface to Book I that you would not be able to tell the time or sing a comic song after using my book. Well, I'm sticking to that for this book, with a couple of minor amendments. First, you will know more about expressions of time than your average grandfather clock after you have finished Chapter 3 of this volume. Secondly, there *is* a little song in Chapter 5, to help you with the perfect passive. Apart from that, however, it's business as usual!

N.R.R.O.

June 1999

GUIDE TO PRONUNCIATION

Vowels

The main problem with learning to pronounce Latin correctly is the vowels. The Romans, as Asterix is always telling us, were crazy and they pronounced their vowels as follows:

ă (short)	as in "cup"	ā (long)	as in "calf"
ĕ (short)	as in "set"	ē (long)	as in "stair"
ĭ (short)	as in "bit"	ī (long)	as in "bee"
ŏ (short)	as in "lot"	ō (long)	as in the French "*beau*"
ŭ (short)	as in "put"	ū (long)	as in "route"

In addition, where the letter y occurs in Latin, it represents the Greek letter *upsilon*, and should be pronounced like a French *u* in words such as "*lune*".

In this book, *long* vowels are marked with a macron (ā, ē, ī, ō, ū). If they are *not* marked, they are short. Occasionally a short vowel is marked as short (ă, ĕ, ĭ, ŏ, ŭ) if there is an incorrect tendency to pronounce the vowel long. For example the o in the Latin word egŏ is marked as short because so many people pronounce the word as if it were long.

Just occasionally a vowel may be marked as being both long *and* short. This is where a vowel is known to have been pronounced long in some places but short in others. In this book, for example, you will come across the words quandŏ and homŏ, the final 'o's of which are sometimes pronounced long, sometimes short. You will also find words such as ubĭ and ibĭ, the final 'i's of which may be either long or short.

A vowel is regularly pronounced long when followed by ns or nf. This rule even applies to the word in when this is followed by a word starting with s or f. E.g. in agrō but īn silvā.

Diphthongs

Where two vowels are pronounced as *one* sound (as in the English *boil*, or *wait*), this is called a **diphthong** and the resulting syllable will always be long. For example the –ae of the word mēnsae is a diphthong. Diphthongs, because they are *always* long, are not marked with a macron.

The most common diphthongs are:

ae	as in "eye"	au	as in "now"

but you may also find:

ei	as in "reign"	oe	as in "boil"
ui	as in French "*oui*"	eu	as in e and u said in one breath!

Vowel and syllable length

You need to learn the quantity of a *vowel* (i.e. whether it is long or short) to ensure that you pronounce the word correctly. But you also need to know the length of the *syllable* that the vowel is in. This is because Latin poetry was based on the subtle combination, not of herbs and spices, but of long and short syllables.

I don't want to put you off before you even start, but you should know that there is a difference between marking a *vowel* as long or short and saying that the syllable itself is long or short. A syllable is long:
(a) if it contains a long vowel or dipthong; or
(b) if it contains a vowel followed by two consonants.
For the purposes of this rule, x and z count as double consonants, as does the consonant i (see below) where this comes between two vowels (see Appendix on page 100). There is an exception to rule (b) which we won't bother with now. Stay tuned for further details.

Consonants

* c is always *hard* as in "cot", never *soft* as in "century".
* ch is always as in "chorus", never as in "chips".
* gn is pronounced ngn, as in "hangnail".
* Latin has no letter j. Instead, the Romans used i as a consonant, pronounced as a y (thus Iūlius Caesar, pronounced Yulius).
* m, at the end of a word, is nasalised and reduced (i.e. only partially pronounced).
* r is always rolled, on the tip of the tongue.
* s is always s as in "bus", never z as in "busy".
* th is always as in "Thomas", never as in "thistle".
* Just as i can be a vowel or a consonant, so it is with u. Consonant u is generally written as a v and is pronounced as a w. In some words, however, it is written as a u, as in the word persuādeō.
* v is in fact a consonant u (see above) and is pronounced as a w.

Stress

Just as in English we have a particular way of stressing words, so they did in Latin. We, for example, say "potáto" (with the stress on the a). When we learn English words, we have to learn how to stress them. For the Romans, there was a simple rule, which could be applied to all words.

The Romans worked out how to stress a word by looking at its penultimate syllable. Syllables, as we have seen, are either long or short. They are long if they contain a long vowel or dipthong, or if they contain a short vowel followed by two consonants. They are short if they contain a short vowel which is *not* followed by two consonants. Using this information, a Latin word should be stressed as follows:

* The final syllable of a word should never be stressed (e.g. ámō, ámās, ámat, etc.).
* In a word of more than two syllables, if the penultimate syllable is long, stress it (e.g. amātis is stressed amátis; amāvístis* is stressed amāvístis).
* If the penultimate syllable is short, stress the the one before it (e.g. regitis is stressed régitis).

* Note how the penultimate syllable of amāvistis is long because the i, although short, is followed by two consonants (st).

INTRODUCTION

We saw in Book I how the Romans came into being: how Aeneas came from Troy and built a city; how his son, Ascanius, built another city, Alba Longa, in which, many generations later, Romulus and Remus were born; and how, after killing his brother, Romulus became king of Rome. We saw, too, how the Romans then had all sorts of adventures, expelling their wicked king, Tarquin the Proud, and fighting off the advances of the Etruscans under their king, Lars Porsenna. In this book we take the story a stage further, seeing how the Romans managed to rise to a position of supremacy in Italy and how they then turned their attention to the people of Carthage. The Roman Empire, as shown on the map below, was still some way off, but it was definitely now on its way.

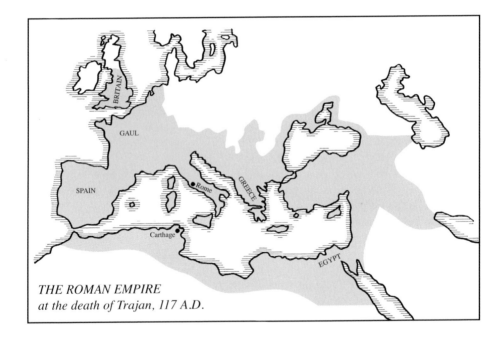

THE ROMAN EMPIRE
at the death of Trajan, 117 A.D.

Translation analysis

Successful translation into or out of Latin is most likely to be achieved if your analysis has been done correctly. Those of you who dive straight into a sentence, grab the first word you see, and try to translate it, will by now have realised that this technique does not often work. The Romans, as you know, had this hideous habit of mucking about with the order of the words, so you can't just take them in the order in which they are written.

In Book I we learnt some Golden Rules for translating and I'm sure you obey these religiously every time you go into action. But let's just see how a sentence should look after you have analysed it, to check that we are all doing the same thing. If you get this bit right, the rest all falls into place like a great big jelly thing. Note how the prepositions and adjectives are always bracketed together with their nouns and the subject, verb and object are always labelled. The remaining words are dealt with carefully, with close attention being paid to the *endings* of the words.

Latin into English

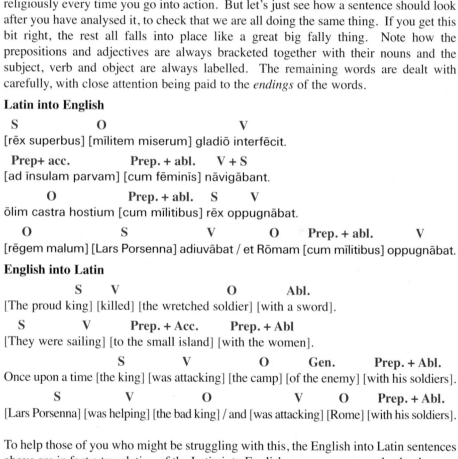

   S   O   V
[rēx superbus] [mīlitem miserum] gladiō interfēcit.

  Prep+ acc.   Prep. + abl.   V + S
[ad īnsulam parvam] [cum fēminīs] nāvigābant.

       O   Prep. + abl.   S   V
ōlim castra hostium [cum mīlitibus] rēx oppugnābat.

   O   S   V   O   Prep. + abl.   V
[rēgem malum] [Lars Porsenna] adiuvābat / et Rōmam [cum mīlitibus] oppugnābat.

English into Latin

           S   V   O   Abl.
[The proud king] [killed] [the wretched soldier] [with a sword].

      S   V   Prep. + Acc.   Prep. + Abl
[They were sailing] [to the small island] [with the women].

          S   V   O   Gen.   Prep. + Abl.
Once upon a time [the king] [was attacking] [the camp] [of the enemy] [with his soldiers].

         S   V   O   V   O   Prep. + Abl.
[Lars Porsenna] [was helping] [the bad king] / and [was attacking] [Rome] [with his soldiers].

To help those of you who might be struggling with this, the English into Latin sentences above are in fact a translation of the Latin into English ones, so you can check what you are doing!

Using Latin

| Vāde mēcum |
| A vāde mēcum is an essential guide or handbook. |
| Vāde mēcum = go with me. |

CHAPTER 1

3rd declension adjectives

Right, here we go then, straight into 3rd declension adjectives. No warm-up. No comforting revision of amō in the present tense. Just straight in.

All the adjectives you have met so far have been 1st/2nd declension (like bonus, tener or pulcher). These adjectives, as you well know, take their endings from the 1st and 2nd declensions. But a large number of adjectives take their endings from the 3rd declension.

One termination adjectives

Some 3rd declension adjectives decline like ingēns:

ingēns, ingentis = huge			
	Masculine	**Feminine**	**Neuter**
Nominative	ingēns	ingēns	ingēns
Vocative	ingēns	ingēns	ingēns
Accusative	ingent-em	ingent-em	ingēns
Genitive	ingent-is	ingent-is	ingent-is
Dative	ingent-ī	ingent-ī	ingent-ī
Ablative	ingent-ī	ingent-ī	ingent-ī
Nominative	ingent-ēs	ingent-ēs	ingent-ia
Vocative	ingent-ēs	ingent-ēs	ingent-ia
Accusative	ingent-ēs	ingent-ēs	ingent-ia
Genitive	ingent-ium	ingent-ium	ingent-ium
Dative	ingent-ibus	ingent-ibus	ingent-ibus
Ablative	ingent-ibus	ingent-ibus	ingent-ibus

Points to note

Adjectives like ingēns have endings taken from the 3rd declension, but the following points should be noted:

1. The endings for the nominative singular are the same for all three genders, and thus ingēns is said to be a *one termination* adjective.
2. One termination adjectives are always listed in the vocabulary with their nominative and genitive singular (e.g. ingēns, ingentis). By taking the genitive singular and chopping off the -is, we are left with the stem. It is to this that the endings (shown above in blue) are added.
3. The ablative singular ends in –ī, not –e.
4. In the plural, ingēns behaves like a non-increasing noun, adding an i to the genitive plural (-ium) and to the first three cases in the neuter (-ia).

So you really want to learn Latin...

Exercise 1. 1
Study the information on the opposite page about third declension adjectives. Notice how "one termination adjectives" are always listed in the vocabulary with their nominative and genitive singular forms. Then translate into English:

1. silvam ingentem vīdimus.
2. mīlitem gladiō ingentī interfēcit.
3. rēx in cubīlī ingentī dormiēbat.
4. tēla ingentia in hostēs iaciēmus.
5. cīvēs audācēs leōnem ingentem nōn timuērunt.

Exercise 1. 2
People tend to go a bit pear-shaped when making 3rd declension adjectives agree with nouns. I can't tell you why, but there is a definite tendency to go pear-shaped. Exactly the same rules apply as for all types of adjective agreement. The noun is written first; then you work out which case, gender and number the noun is; then you put the adjective into that form.
   E.g. of the farmer:
   Masculine, genitive singular
   = agricolae
   Of the *huge* farmer
   = agricolae ingentis

Translate into Latin:

1. Of the huge table
2. Of the huge tables
3. The bold girl (nom.)
4. The bold girls (acc.)
5. Towards the huge wood
6. With the bold soldiers
7. Without a bold leader
8. The huge camp (nom.)
9. Under the huge table
10. With the bold sailor

Exercise 1. 3
Translate into English:

1. cōpiae Rōmānae castra Etruscōrum prope flūmen ingēns oppugnābant.
2. Etruscī autem castra ingentia prope flūmen parāvērunt.
3. Lars Porsenna, rēx Etruscōrum, mīlitēs audācēs ad Rōmānōs dūxit.
4. Rōmānī autem hostēs audācēs nōn timēbant et in pugnam festīnāvērunt.
5. Etruscī Rōmānōs audācēs vīdērunt nec tamen fugere cupiēbant.

Using Latin

C.V.
The letters C.V. stand for curriculum vītae
= course of life.

Two termination adjectives

You have now met a 3rd declension adjective and realised how easy it was. But most 3rd declension adjectives are not one termination, like ingēns, but *two termination*, like trīstis:

trīstis, trīste = sad, gloomy

	Masculine	Feminine	Neuter
Nominative	trīstis	trīstis	trīst-e
Vocative	trīstis	trīstis	trīst-e
Accusative	trīst-em	trīst-em	trīst-e
Genitive	trīst-is	trīst-is	trīst-is
Dative	trīst-ī	trīst-ī	trīst-ī
Ablative	trīst-ī	trīst-ī	trīst-ī
Nominative	trīst-ēs	trīst-ēs	trīst-ia
Vocative	trīst-ēs	trīst-ēs	trīst-ia
Accusative	trīst-ēs	trīst-ēs	trīst-ia
Genitive	trīst-ium	trīst-ium	trīst-ium
Dative	trīst-ibus	trīst-ibus	trīst-ibus
Ablative	trīst-ibus	trīst-ibus	trīst-ibus

Points to note

1. Trīstis is said to be two termination because in the nominative singular it has two different endings, one for the masculine and feminine, and one for the neuter.
2. To show that it is a two termination adjective, the two nominative singular forms are given (trīstis, trīste). This is often abbreviated to trīstis, -e.
3. The stem of two termination adjectives can be found by going to the neuter form (trīste) and chopping off the –e.

Three termination adjectives

A small number of adjectives are said to be *three termination*, because in the nominative singular they have *three* different endings. E.g. ācer, ācris, ācre = keen, or celer, celeris, celere = swift. They decline exactly like trīstis, except for the fact that they have different masculine and feminine endings in the nominative and vocative singular.

	M	F	N
Nom.	ācer	ācris	ācre
Voc.	ācer	ācris	ācre
Acc.	ācrem	ācrem	ācre
Etc.			

Adjectives like this would originally have ended in -is in the nominative masculine singular, but at some stage in the dim and distant past the word seems to have changed. Notice also that some of these adjectives (e.g. ācer) drop their e, while others (e.g. celer) do not.

So you really want to learn Latin...

Exercise 1. 4

Study the information on the opposite page about 3rd declension adjectives like trīstis. Most 3rd declension adjectives decline like this, so make sure you are thoroughly familiar with it. Write out in full (all three genders, all cases, singular and plural):

1. brevis, breve = short, brief
2. fēlīx, fēlīcis = fortunate
3. celer, celeris, celere = swift

Exercise 1. 5

Translate into Latin:

1. Of the sad king
2. To the sad farmer
3. With the sad soldier
4. In the sad poem
5. O sad girls
6. Under the heavy book
7. In the short letter
8. The easy victories (nom.)
9. Of the brave leader
10. The difficult song (nom.)

Exercise 1. 6

Translate into English:

1. puella epistolam brevem ad magistrum mīsit.
2. dux fortis multōs mīlitēs in pugnam difficilem dūcēbat.
3. puerī et puellae dē colle currēbant.
4. herī incolae Ītaliae erant trīstēs.
5. carmina trīstia iam cantat.
6. dux trīstis cōpiās fortēs in mare dūxerat.
7. nostrī* in marī diū pugnābant nec tamen nautās superābant.
8. māter trīstis fīliam laetam sub mēnsā invēnit.
9. cūr aquam ē marī ad urbem portātis?
10. multōs clāmōrēs īn silvīs audiēbant.

*Adjectives are often used without a noun. Nostrī (in the masculine) = "our men". Nostrae would mean "our women" and nostra would mean "our things".

Using Latin

Annus horribilis
If one has had a really bad year, one may describe it as an annus horribilis = terrible year.

Page 10

dum + historic present

dum = "while" is most often followed by a *present* tense in Latin, where in English we would expect an *imperfect*. The rule about this is one of my favourites (partly because it allows us to use the word coterminous) and is as follows:

- dum is followed by a historic present in Latin where it refers to a period of time, *during the course of which something else happens*.
  E.g. while we were walking, we found a horse =
  dum ambulāmus, equum invēnimus.
- But if dum refers to a period of time which is *coterminous with the thing happening*, then an imperfect is used.
  E.g. while we were walking, we were singing =
  dum ambulābāmus, cantābāmus.
  In this example, all the time that we were walking we were singing, thus the two activities were coterminous.

Vocabulary 1

Adjectives		Nouns	
audāx, audācis	bold	cīvis, cīvis, c.	citizen
brevis, breve	short, brief	collis, collis, m.	hill
celer, celeris, celere	swift	dolor, dolōris, m.	pain, grief
difficilis, difficile	difficult	mare, maris, n.	sea
facilis, facile	easy	**Verbs**	
fortis, forte	brave, strong	inveniō, -īre, invēnī, inventum	I find
gravis, grave	serious, heavy		
ingēns, ingentis	huge	iubeō, iubēre, iussī, iussum	I order
laetus, -a, -um	happy		
trīstis, trīste	sad, gloomy	laudō, -āre, -āvī, -ātum	I praise
Adverbs			
herī	yesterday	**Conjunction**	
hodiē	today	igitur (never 1st word)	therefore

Reminder to the modern linguists

Don't forget to keep looking for similarities between Latin and the modern languages. For example, take a squint at this lot. I particularly like herī = "yesterday", even though there is no English derivation. Say the word herī a million times very quickly, and you will understand how it came to be pronounced in such different ways in these different languages.

Latin	facilis	difficilis	gravis	herī	mare
English	facility	difficult	grave	–	marine
French	facile	difficile	grave	hier	mer
Spanish	facil	dificil	grave	ayer	mar
Italian	facile	difficile	grave	ieri	mare

So you really want to learn Latin...

Exercise 1. 7

Study the information on the opposite page about dum and the historic present. Then translate the story of the escape of Cloelia, 508 B.C. Underlined words are given below.

dum rēx Porsenna Rōmam oppugnat, multās puellās cēpit. puella, nōmine Cloelia, fugere cupiēbat. trāns flūmen igitur cum amīcīs <u>natāvit</u> et in urbem ambulāvit. Porsenna autem īrātus erat et mīlitēs ad Rōmānōs mīsit. "ubĭ est Cloelia?" rogāvērunt. Rōmānī autem <u>foedus</u> cum Porsennā fēcerant neque foedus <u>violāre</u> cupiēbant. Cloeliam igitur miseram ad castra Porsennae <u>remīsērunt</u>. Porsenna tamen nōn īrātus sed laetus erat. "Rōmānī" inquit "fortēs sunt et <u>dignī</u> fāmā. Cloeliam igitur, et multās puellās, Rōmānīs dabō."

natō, -āre = I swim; foedus, -eris, n. = treaty; violō, -āre = I violate; remittō = I send back; dignus, -a, -um + ablative = worthy. This adjective is followed by an ablative in Latin, where in English we use a genitive (i.e. "worthy *of*").

Exercise 1. 8

Translate into Latin:

1. O bold leaders!
2. Of the swift girl
3. By a brave soldier
4. For the serious work
5. In the deep sea

6. He has seen the sad women
7. The happy farmer was singing
8. He wanted to see the sad girl
9. Down from the high hill
10. He will tell a short story

Exercise 1. 9

Study the reminder to modern linguists on the opposite page. Amazing, isn't it? Now, putting on your beret and stripy t-shirt, say from which Latin words these *French* ones derive. Translate the Latin words and give the meaning of the French ones.

1. appeler
2. arbre
3. bon
4. pont
5. dormir
6. descendre
7. et
8. habiter
9. mal
10. audacieux

Using Latin

Crux
The *crux* of the matter is the difficult bit. In Latin, crux = a cross (on which criminals were crucified).

Coriolanus

The story of Coriolanus is said to date from a time when Rome was suffering from famine and a spate of attacks from a neighbouring tribe called the Volsci. In 493 B.C., the Roman general Gnaeus Marcius captured the Volscian town of Corioli and thus acquired the name Coriolanus. However, he became proud and tyrannical and, when he opposed the distribution of corn to the starving poor, he was driven from the city. Ironically, he sought refuge with the Volsci and, in 491, he marched on Rome at the head of a Volscian army.

Enter, stage left, the mother, wife and small children of Coriolanus. Disgusted at the treachery of her son, Coriolanus's mother stormed into the enemy camp and, indicating his wife and children, demanded to know whether her son intended to kill them, too. The poor chap couldn't cope with this and skulked away, reappearing two thousand years later in a play by Shakespeare.

So you really want to learn Latin...

Exercise 1. 10

Read the story of Coriolanus on the opposite page. Then translate into English:

ōlim Rōmānī cum Volscīs bellum gerēbant. oppidum autem nōmine Coriolōs oppugnāvērunt nec tamen cēpērunt. tandem Gnaeus Mārcius, mīles Rōmānus, cōpiās in oppidum dūxit et multōs hostēs interfēcit. Rōmānī audācēs Volscōs miserōs superāvērunt et nōmen novum Mārciō dedērunt: iam Gnaeus Mārcius Coriolānus erat.

Exercise 1. 11

Translate into Latin:

For a long time the Romans were fearing Coriolanus. At last they compelled the proud soldier to depart from the city. He fled to the camp of the Volsci and he fought against the Romans. Therefore the mother and wife of Coriolanus came into the camp of the enemy. "Why are you attacking your city?" the mother asked. Coriolanus heard the words of his mother and departed with his soldiers. Then the Romans praised the bold women.

Revision

Write down and learn by heart:

* Ingēns.
* Trīstis.
* Ācer.
* The words in Vocabulary 1.

Using Latin

Compos mentis

Compos mentis = "possessing a mind", i.e. sane.

CHAPTER 2
Pronouns

Personal pronouns

So far you have coped without pronouns, relying on the verb ending to tell you who is doing the verb. But there are times when you *need* pronouns:
1. For emphasis: *We* are awake but *you* are sleeping.
2. When we wish the pronoun to be the object, or to be in the genitive, dative or ablative case: The farmer sees *you*; we give the book *to you*, etc.

The pronouns of the 1st and 2nd persons decline as follows:

	1st person		2nd person	
Nom.	egŏ	I	tū	You (sing.)
Voc.	-	-	tū	O you!
Acc.	mē	Me	tē	You
Gen.	meī	Of me	tuī	Of you
Dat.	mihĭ	To, for me	tibĭ	To, for you
Abl.	mē	With, by, from me	tē	With, by, from you
Nom.	nōs	We	vōs	You (pl.)
Voc.	-	-	vōs	O you!
Acc.	nōs	Us	vōs	You
Gen.	nostrum/nostrī	Of us	vestrum/vestrī	Of you
Dat.	nōbīs	To, for us	vōbīs	To, for you
Abl.	nōbīs	With, by, from us	vōbīs	With, by, from you

Points to note

Problems can arise with the words nōs and vōs unless you are careful.
1. If the verb is 1st person plural, nōs = "we" and is used for emphasis. If the verb is anything other than 1st person plural, nōs must mean "us".
   E.g. nōs spectāmus = *we* are watching; but
   nōs spectant = they are watching *us*.
2. The same applies for vōs. If the verb is 2nd person plural, vōs = "you" (nominative or, possibly, vocative) and is used for emphasis. If it is anything else, vōs must be accusative.
   E.g. vōs spectātis = *you* are watching; but
   vōs spectant = they are watching *you*.
3. The genitive of personal pronouns is not often found, because instead of "of me" we usually say "my", instead of "of you" we say "your", etc. However, the two different forms for "of us" and "of you (pl.)" do need to be distinguished. Nostrum and vestrum are said to be **partitive genitives**, because they are used after words which express a part (e.g. ūnus nostrum = one of us). Nostrī and vestrī are **objective genitives**, used after nouns and adjectives in which a verbal notion is prominent (e.g. love of us = amor nostrī).

So you really want to learn Latin...

Exercise 2. 1

Study the information on the opposite page about personal pronouns. Then translate into Latin:

1. To you (sing.)
2. To me
3. We see you
4. You see us
5. He watches you (pl.)

6. *You* sleep but *we* work
7. I give the book to you (sing.)
8. He heard me
9. They will warn us
10. I will praise you (sing.)

Exercise 2. 2

Translate into English:

1. cīvēs mē audiēbant.
2. mīles celer nōs spectābit.
3. herī tē vidēre cupiēbam.
4. mare nōs amāmus sed tū timēs.
5. hodiē mīlitēs audācēs vōs capient.
6. ō Rōmānī, ecce, Rōmulus in caelum ascendit!
7. Lars Porsenna multōs captīvōs cēpit.
8. māter mea tēcum* ambulat.
9. nōs legimus sed tū dormīs.
10. nōs dōna tibī dedimus.

> * When using the preposition cum = "with", it is *joined on* to the ablative of the personal pronouns as follows: mēcum = with me, tēcum = with you, nōbīscum = with us, vōbīscum = with you (pl.).

Exercise 2. 3

Translate into Latin:

1. Coriolanus has attacked our city.
2. Perhaps Coriolanus's dear mother will enter the camp of the enemy.
3. Your mother does not love you, Coriolanus.
4. Look, she has come within our camp!
5. Does your love of us compel you to attack Rome?
6. I will not capture you but I will depart.
7. Therefore Coriolanus departed from the camp.
8. However his mother was not happy.
9. The Romans saw the tears of the sad mother.
10. She had loved the boy, but in vain.

Using Latin

Pāx vōbīscum
Pāx vōbīscum = peace (be) with you.

Is, Ea, Id

So, coping with "I" and "you" and "we" and "us" is pretty easy. But what about "him" and "her" and "them"? Here a mini problem occurs: there is no 3rd person pronoun in Latin. Instead Latin uses the demonstrative pronoun "that": it uses it in the masculine to mean "he", in the feminine to mean "she" and in the neuter to mean "it".

is, ea, id = *that (he, she, it)*

	Singular			Plural		
	M	**F**	**N**	**M**	**F**	**N**
Nom.	is	ea	id	eī/iī	eae	ea
Voc.	-	-	-	-	-	-
Acc.	eum	eam	id	eōs	eās	ea
Gen.	eius	eius	eius	eōrum	eārum	eōrum
Dat.	eī	eī	eī	eīs/iīs	eīs/iīs	eīs/iīs
Abl.	eō	eā	eō	eīs/iīs	eīs/iīs	eīs/iīs

The genitive singular eius is pronounced as if spelt eiius. The e is short, but the first syllable counts as a long syllable and should be lingered over. See Appendix on page 100 (note 4).

Using is, ea, id

Generally, is, ea, id means "that" **when used in agreement with a noun**. When used alone it means "he", "she" or "it".

E.g. agricola eum puerum videt = the farmer sees that boy.

E.g. agricola eum videt = The farmer sees him.

Translating his, her, its and their

1. So far we have managed to translate "his", "her", "its" or "their" by leaving the words out altogether!

   E.g. puer mātrem amat = the boy loves his mother.

2. If, however, we wish to stress or emphasise the fact that by "his" we mean "his own", or by "their" we mean "their own" etc., we use suus, -a, -um.

   E.g. she sees her (own) brother = suum frātrem videt.

   E.g. they see their (own) mother = suam mātrem vident.

3. Finally, if by "his" we mean "someone else's", we use the genitive of is, ea, id.

   E.g. she sees his (i.e. someone else's) friend = eius amīcum videt.

   E.g. she sees their (i.e. not her) mother = eōrum mātrem videt.

Transitive and intransitive verbs

A transitive verb is one which governs a direct object in the accusative case (e.g. agricolam vulnerat). An intransitive verb is one which does not govern a direct object (e.g. ambulō = I walk). Some intransitive verbs govern an *indirect object* in the dative case. E.g. crēdō + dative = I trust; persuādeō + dative = I persuade.

E.g. I trust you = tibĭ crēdō; I persuade the Romans = Rōmānīs persuādeō.

So you really want to learn Latin...

Exercise 2. 4
Study the information on the opposite page about is, ea, id. Note also what it says about transitive and intransitive verbs and verbs followed by the dative. Then give the Latin for:

1. We love him
2. You (sing.) love her
3. She trusts them
4. We love it
5. For him

6. With them
7. Without her
8. She
9. It (nom.)
10. *He* loves *her*

Exercise 2. 5
Translate into Latin:

1. To me
2. From you (sing.)
3. Of him
4. Those soldiers (nom.)
5. For them
6. For you (pl.)
7. With us
8. Me
9. Him
10. For her

Exercise 2. 6
Translate into English:

1. dōnum tibĭ dedī
2. nōbīs dōna dedit
3. māter eius
4. id flūmen
5. nōs monētis
6. mēnsam eius parābō
7. ad eum epistolam mittam
8. eam epistolam legit
9. vōs ambulātis
10. num nōbīs crēdis?

Exercise 2. 7
Read the information on the left-hand page about translating "his", "her", "its", and "their". Then translate into Latin:

1. She loves her mother.
2. They love their country.
3. She loves his mother.
4. They love her country.
5. We praise you but we do not like him.
6. You praise us but you do not like them.
7. They praise them but they do not like you.
8. He loves that girl.

Usĭng Latin	**Egŏ** If one has a big *ego*, one thinks a great deal of oneself. Egŏ = I.

Vocabulary 2

Nouns

caelum, caelī, n.	sky
captīvus, captīvī, m.	prisoner
iuvenis, iuvenis, c.	young person/man
lacrima, lacrimae, f.	tear

Verbs

adiuvō, adiuvāre, adiūvī, adiūtum	I help
intrō, intrāre, intrāvī, intrātum	I enter
crēdō, crēdere, crēdidī, crēditum + dat.	I trust, I believe
dēscendō, -ere, dēscendī, dēscēnsum	I go down
legō, legere, lēgī, lēctum	I read, choose

Adjectives

cārus, -a, -um	dear
fidēlis, fidēle	faithful
suus, -a, -um	his, her, its or their (own)

Adverbs

fortasse	perhaps
frūstrā	in vain
ibĭ	there
inde	then, thence
ita	thus

Conjunction

itaque	therefore

Prepositions

intrā + acc.	within
trāns + acc.	across

Prefixes

We saw in Book I how Latin prepositions are often used as English prefixes. Here are some of the most common English prefixes, most of which you have now met as Latin prepositions:

a(b)-	from	di(s)-	apart	pre-	in front of
ad-	to	e(x)-	out of	pro-	forward
circum-	around	in-*	in, on, into, not	re-	back, again
co(n)-	together	inter-	between	se-	apart
contra-	against	intro-	within	sub-	under
de-	down, from	per-	through	trans-	across

*N.B. *in* can mean "in" or "into", but it can also make the word negative, as in "inaudible". Note how many of these prefixes may change slightly in front of different letters, to make them easier to say. For example con- (which comes from the Latin cum) often becomes col- or com-, in- becomes il-, ob- becomes op-, sub- becomes sup-, etc.

Revision

So how are we doing? Here's what we should know:

- All regular verbs plus sum in the six tenses.
- Regular nouns of the first three declensions.
- Irregular nouns: fīlius, deus and vir.
- Cardinals 1–20 and ordinals 1st–10th.
- Bonus, tener and pulcher.
- Ingēns and trīstis.
- Egŏ, tū, nōs and vōs.
- Is, ea, id.
- Vocabularies 1-10 in Book I.
- Vocabularies 1-2 in this book.

So you really want to learn Latin...

Exercise 2. 8
Study the words in Vocabulary 2 and the list of prefixes on the opposite page. Note that con- comes from the Latin cum. Note also how prefixes may change their spelling to make the word easier to say. From which Latin words do the following derive? Translate the Latin words and explain the meaning of the English ones.

1. Frustrate
2. Concurred
3. Discredit
4. Captive
5. Descent
6. Illegible
7. Juvenile
8. Infidelity
9. Lecture
10. Introspective

Exercise 2. 9
Practice with prefixes. Which English words do we get from the following and what do they mean? Note any changes to the spelling of the prefix.

1. contrā and veniō
2. contrā and dīcō
3. circum and spectō
4. in and audiō
5. inter and iaciō
6. dis and pellō
7. re and pellō
8. in and pellō
9. ex and pellō
10. cum* and pellō

* N.B. cum becomes com-, con- or co- when used as a prefix.

Exercise 2. 10
Translate into English:

1. rēx captīvōs miserōs ad urbem suam mīsit.
2. dominī multōs servōs īn forum dūxērunt.
3. fīlia mīlitis intrā mūrōs vēnit.
4. fortasse hostēs intrā urbem dūcere cupiēbat.
5. hostēs tamen puellae miserae nōn crēdidērunt.

Exercise 2. 11
Read the points for revision on the opposite page. Then write out the following, without looking up:

1. capiō in the present, future and imperfect.
2. cīvis in the singular and plural.
3. The ordinals 1st – 10th.
4. sum in the present, future and imperfect.

Using Latin

I.V.F.
"Test-tube babies" are born as a result of in vitrō fertilisiation. In vitrō = in glass.

The story of Verginia, 449 B.C.

In the early days of the Roman republic there was a constant conflict between the patricians (the aristocratic families descended from the original founders of Rome) and the plebeians (the common citizens). A major grievance of the plebeians was that the laws were not written down, so nobody knew what one was allowed to do. In about 450 B.C., ten judges were appointed to study the laws of Athens and then write down a set of laws for Rome. These came to be known as the Twelve Tables.

One of these judges was a man called Appius Claudius. He caused something of a scandal when he tried to use his power as a judge to get hold of a girl called Verginia, despite the fact that she was already betrothed to another man. He persuaded a friend of his, Marcus Claudius, to claim that Verginia was a slave-girl belonging to him. Marcus brought her to court and the judge in the case was none other than Appius Claudius. When the girl's father realised that his daughter was going to be taken from him and given over to the wicked judge, he saw no other way to rescue her from such a dreadful fate: he drew his sword and killed her.

So you really want to learn Latin...

Exercise 2. 12
Read the story of Verginia on the opposite page. Then answer the questions in complete sentences:

1. Who were the patricians?
2. Who were the plebeians?
3. What was the grievance that the plebeians had against the patricians?
4. What were the ten judges appointed to do in c. 450 B.C.?
5. What was the name given to the set of laws they produced?
6. Who was Appius Claudius?
7. Who was Verginia and why was it inappropriate for Appius Claudius to be chasing after her?
8. Describe Appius Claudius's plan for laying his hands on Verginia.
9. What did Verginia's father do when he realised he was powerless to protect his daughter?
10. What does this story tell us about the Roman character?

Exercise 2. 13
Translate into English: *A Roman father saves his daughter.*

ōlim cīvis Rōmānus, nōmine Appius Claudius, puellam pulchram, nōmine Vergīniam, amābat. sed pater Vergīniae eam in <u>mātrimōnium</u> iam prōmīserat. Appius igitur amīcō suō "nōnne tū" inquit "mē adiuvābis? eam puellam <u>in mātrimōnium dūcere</u> cupiō." amīcus eius forum intrāvit et Vergīniam cēpit. ea autem fugere cupiēbat sed frūstrā. pater tamen fīliam vīdit et clāmāvit. "fīliam meam" inquit "nōn capiēs. eam servābō." inde gladium cēpit et fīliam cāram interfēcit. ita puellam miseram servāvit.

mātrimōnium, -iī, n. = marriage; in mātrimōnium dūcō = I lead into marriage, I marry.

Using Latin	**Avē Maria** Avē Maria are the opening words of a famous prayer of the Roman Catholic Church. Avē Maria = Hail Mary!

CHAPTER 3
The 4th declension; imperatives; declining numerals; expressions of time

4th declension nouns

Most 4th declension nouns decline like gradus and are almost all masculine. A few neuter ones exist, which decline like genū. Neuter nouns of the 4th declension are not wildly common, but they are such fun that they are shown here for the sake of light relief from the stresses of modern living.

	gradus, -ūs, m. = step		genū, genūs, n. = knee	
	Singular	**Plural**	**Singular**	**Plural**
Nominative	grad-us	grad-ūs	gen-ū	gen-ua
Vocative	grad-us	grad-ūs	gen-ū	gen-ua
Accusative	grad-um	grad-ūs	gen-ū	gen-ua
Genitive	grad-ūs	grad-uum	gen-ūs	gen-uum
Dative	grad-uī	grad-ibus	gen-ū	gen-ibus
Ablative	grad-ū	grad-ibus	gen-ū	gen-ibus

Points to note

- 4th declension nouns are a nightmare, because they look like 2nd declension nouns in the nominative singular, but then go completely pear-shaped. You can tell that they are 4th declension by the genitive singular in –ūs (rhyming with *juice*).
- Extreme care needs to be taken when translating Latin which contains 4th declension nouns, due to the fact that the –us ending of the nominative and vocative singular can easily be confused with the –ūs ending which occurs no less than four times.
- All the 4th declension nouns in –us that you meet in this book are masculine except manus = "hand" and domus = "house" which are feminine.
- Occasionally, -ubus is found instead of -ibus in the dative and ablative plural.

Irregular 4th declension noun: domus

The Latin for a "house" or "home" is irregular, taking its endings from the 2nd and 4th declensions almost at random. Rarer forms are given in brackets.

	domus, domūs, f. = house	
	Singular	**Plural**
Nominative	dom-us	dom-ūs
Vocative	dom-us	dom-ūs
Accusative	dom-um	dom-ōs (dom-ūs)
Genitive	dom-ūs	dom-uum (dom-ōrum)
Dative	dom-uī (dom-ō)	dom-ibus
Ablative	dom-ō	dom-ibus

So you really want to learn Latin...

Exercise 3. 1

Study the information on the opposite page about 4th declension nouns. Note the way that 2nd and 4th declension nouns can be distinguished by looking at their genitive singular: 2nd declension nouns go -ī, 4th declension nouns go -ūs. Then decline in full:

1. manus, manūs, f. = hand
2. exercitus, exercitūs, m. = army
3. cornū, cornūs, n. = horn, wing (of an army)
4. oculus, oculī, m. = eye

Exercise 3. 2

Translate into Latin:

1. He will lead the army towards the harbour.
2. The leader of the army was a brave soldier.
3. The enemy were defending the homes of the inhabitants.
4. All the old men were sitting on the steps.
5. Yesterday my father gave a huge horn to the good slave.
6. He sat on the step of the house because the soldiers had wounded his knee.
7. The leader of the barbarians was fighting on the left wing.
8. We will lead the armies towards the river.

Exercise 3. 3

Translate into English:

1. dominus servī domum novam eī dedit.
2. nostrī in campō sagittīs et gladiīs pugnābant.
3. dux exercitūs mīlitēs in montēs dūxit.
4. captīvōs in portū tenēbāmus.
5. omnēs servī ex hortō veniēbant et ad portum currēbant.
6. vōs dē montibus ambulātis sed nōs currimus.
7. num domōs prope portum aedificābitis?
8. nōnne dux exercitūs aestātem amat?

Exercise 3. 4

Now for some hairy Gauls! Translate into English: *The Battle of Allia, 390 B.C.*

ōlim Rōmānī contrā Gallōs bellum gerēbant. rēx Gallōrum, nōmine Brennus, exercitum ad urbem dūxit et cum Rōmānīs prope flūmen, nōmine Alliam, pugnāre parāvit. Rōmānī tamen Gallōs vīdērunt et in urbem statim fūgērunt. tum Gallī ad urbem vēnērunt et domōs cīvium intrāvērunt.

	Cōgitō, ergǒ sum
Using Latin	This famous phrase, coined by the 17th century French philosopher, Descartes, means "I think, therefore I am".

The imperative

Commands are given using the imperative. The imperative of a verb is formed from the present stem and may be singular or plural, as shown:

Sing.	amā	monē	reg-ĕ	audī	cap-ĕ
Plural	amā-te	monē-te	reg-ĭte	audī-te	cap-ĭte
	Love!	Warn!	Rule!	Listen!	Capture!

1. These are pretty straightforward, with only regō and capiō causing problems. Regō adds -e in the singular but -ĭte in the plural, just to be difficult, and capiō copies regō.
2. The following verbs have irregular imperatives:
   faciō: fac / facite = do! dīcō: dīc / dīcite = say!
   dūcō: dūc / dūcite = lead! sum: es / este = be!
3. The final ē of the imperative of caveō (= I beware) is often shortened to ĕ.

Declining numerals

As we have already seen, the ordinal numerals are adjectives and decline like bonus.
E.g. the first girl = puella prīma.
E.g. the first war = bellum prīmum.
But the cardinals "one", "two" and "three" also decline in Latin as follows, with ūnus having both a singular and plural:

	Singular Masc.	Fem.	Neut.	Plural Masc.	Fem.	Neut.
Nom.	ūnus	ūna	ūnum	ūnī	ūnae	ūna
Acc.	ūnum	ūnam	ūnum	ūnōs	ūnās	ūna
Gen.	ūnĭus	ūnĭus	ūnĭus	ūnōrum	ūnārum	ūnōrum
Dat.	ūnī	ūnī	ūnī	ūnīs	ūnīs	ūnīs
Abl.	ūnō	ūnā	ūnō	ūnīs	ūnīs	ūnīs

	Masc.	Fem.	Neut.	Masc.	Fem.	Neut.
Nom.	duŏ	duae	duŏ	trēs	trēs	tria
Acc.	duōs/duŏ	duās	duŏ	trēs	trēs	tria
Gen.	duōrum	duārum	duōrum	trium	trium	trium
Dat.	duōbus	duābus	duōbus	tribus	tribus	tribus
Abl.	duōbus	duābus	duōbus	tribus	tribus	tribus

N.B. It may at first appear odd that ūnus = "one" has a plural! This is because, when used in agreement with a plural noun, it has to be plural. Note also that, as well as meaning "one", ūnus also means "one alone" or "only one".
E.g. ūna castra = "one camp" or "only one camp".
E.g. ūnae cōpiae = "the one (set of) forces".
Several other Latin words decline like ūnus, so make sure you learn it!

So you really want to learn Latin...

Exercise 3. 5
Read the information on the opposite page about imperatives. Note that you can tell whether the imperative is singular or plural by looking at who is being addressed. Now give the Latin for:

1. Sail into the harbour, sailors!
2. Be brave, soldiers!
3. Sit on the step, boy!
4. Listen to* all the stories, boys!
5. Lead the army into war, Coriolanus!

*N.B. audiō = "I hear" or "I listen *to*". It is thus followed by an accusative, not a dative.

Exercise 3. 6
Read the information on the opposite page about declining numerals. Then translate into Latin:

1. Of the fourth girl
2. With the third sword
3. To the fifth boy
4. The second war (nom.)
5. The tenth year (nom.)
6. With three friends
7. With the sixth king
8. The one* camp
9. The only* forces (nom.)
10. Of one farmer

* Use ūnus in plural.

Exercise 3. 7
Translate into English:

1. patrēs Rōmānī filiōs semper docēbant.
2. multās fābulās eīs nārrābant.
3. rēx prīmus, nōmine Rōmulus, Rōmam regēbat.
4. septem rēgēs urbem regēbant.
5. eōs tamen Rōmānī nōn amābant quod superbī erant.
6. Brūtus rēgem ex urbe pepulit et diū Rōmam dēfendēbat.
7. Lars Porsenna cum exercitū magnō pontem dēlēre cupiēbat.
8. Horātius cum duōbus amīcīs pontem diū dēfendēbat et urbem servāvit.
9. inde duŏ cōnsulēs urbem regēbant.
10. iuvenēs Rōmānī senēs audiēbant et eōs semper timēbant.

Using Latin	**Cavĕ canem** Cavĕ canem = beware of the dog!

Towns, small islands...

There is a wonderful rule about towns, small islands, domus and rūs:

> When going to or from *towns, small islands,* domus or rūs you must **not** use a preposition.

This rule applies to *the names of* towns (Rome, Troy, etc.); *the names of* small islands (Ithaca, Rhodes, etc.); domus = home; and rūs, rūris, n. = the countryside. It does not apply to the word "town" itself (i.e. oppidum), or to the words īnsula parva = "small island". It is only *named* towns or small islands.

Thus, if you are walking *"to* Rome", Rōmam ambulās. Rome goes in the accusative, as it would have done after the preposition ad, but the ad is not used. Similarly, if you are walking *"from* Rome", Rōmā ambulās, where Rome is in the ablative as it would have been after the preposition ā/ab.

Thus:

He walks home from Troy = domum Troiā ambulat.

He walks to the country = rūs ambulat.

He sails from Ithaca to Sicily = Ithacā ad Siciliam nāvigat.

(In this last example, Ithaca is classed as a small island, whereas Sicily is not.)

But (of course):

He walks to the town = **ad** oppidum ambulat.

He sails to the small island = **ad** īnsulam parvam nāvigat.

If, by the way, a preposition *is* used, it means "to the neighbourhood of...".

E.g. ad Rōmam ambulō = I am walking to the neighbourhood of Rome.

Vocabulary 3

Nouns

aestās, aestātis, f.	summer	rūs, rūris, n.	countryside
campus, campī, m.	plain	senex, senis, m.	old man
domus, -ūs, f.	house, home	**Verbs**	
exercitus, -ūs, m.	army	dēfendō, dēfendere,	I defend
hōra, hōrae, f.	hour	dēfendī, dēfēnsum	
ignis, ignis, m.	fire	discō, discere, didicī	I learn
imperātor,	general	pōnō, pōnere, posuī,	I place, pitch
imperātōris, m.		positum	(a camp)
iter, itineris, n.	journey	**Adjective**	
lūna, lūnae, f.	moon	omnis, omne	all, every
mōns, montis, m.	mountain	**Conjunction**	
pāx, pācis, f.	peace	quod	because
pecūnia, -ae, f.	money	**Adverb**	
portus, -ūs, m.	harbour	semper	always

So you really want to learn Latin...

Exercise 3. 8
Read the rule about towns, small islands, etc. on the opposite page. Then translate into English:

1. domum ambulābat.
2. Troiā discesserant.
3. Rōmam festīnābant.
4. Ithacam nāvigābimus.
5. nōnne ā Crētā nāvigāvistis?

6. ad oppidum ambulāmus.
7. ad īnsulam nāvigābat.
8. rūs ex urbe festīnābam.
9. domum rūre festīnābat.
10. Troiam nāvigāvērunt.

Exercise 3. 9
Translate into English: *The Gauls enter Rome, 390 B.C.*

Gallī autem urbem intrāvērunt quod incolae eōs timēbant. fēminae et iuvenēs in montem Capitōlium ascenderant sed senēs īn forō sedēbant. Gallī īn forum ambulāvērunt et diū eōs spectābant. senēs Rōmānī nihil faciēbant. tandem Gallus senem Rōmānum tetigit et is īrātus erat. inde Gallus eum interfēcit et amīcī eius omnēs Rōmānōs interfēcērunt. mīlitēs autem nōn invēnērunt quod eī in monte cum fēminīs manēbant.

diū Rōmānī in monte manēbant. tandem Gallī montem ascendērunt. mīlitēs Rōmānī eōs nōn audīvērunt. sed ānserēs sacrī Gallōs audīvērunt et clāmāvērunt. mīlitēs surrēxērunt et hostēs dē monte pepulērunt.

tangō, tangere, tetigī, tāctum = I touch; ānser, ānseris, m. = goose; sacer, sacra, sacrum = sacred

Exercise 3. 10
From which Latin words do the following derive? Translate the Latin word and explain the meaning of the English one:

1. Lunatic
2. Senile
3. Pacified
4. Impecunious
5. Position

6. Ignite
7. Defence
8. Lunar
9. Hostile
10. Insular

Using Latin

Omnibus
The word *bus* is short for omnibus = "for all". The first bus was designed to provide transport *for all.*

Expressions of time

Expressions of time in Latin are expressed according to the rules of the following silly rhyme:

> Expressions of time you may learn by this rhyme,
> Prepositions you never must use;
> "Within which" and "when": use the ablative case,
> But for time "how long": use the accus.*
> * (-ative).

This is all very well, but, apart from the fact that it doesn't even rhyme properly, what does it all mean?

1. If you wish to describe **when** something happened, you use the ablative case.
    E.g. In the second year = secundō annō.
    E.g. On the third day = tertiō diē.

2. If you wish to describe a period of time **within which**, or **during which** something happened, again you must use the ablative case.
    E.g. Within three days = tribus diēbus.
    E.g. During the third hour = tertiā hōrā.
    N.B. in the expression "by night" or "during the night", noctū is regularly used instead of nocte.

3. If you wish to describe the duration of a period of time, i.e. say **how long** it lasted, you use the accusative case. Occasionally the preposition per is used.
    E.g. For two years = duōs annōs.
    E.g. For many days = (per) multōs diēs.

4. If you wish to say **how long ago** something happened, you use the adverb abhinc, normally with the accusative (less commonly with the ablative).
    E.g. Two years ago = abhinc duōs annōs.

5. If you wish to say **how long before** or **how long after**, you use ante or post as adverbs, putting the period of time into the ablative case. These adverbs normally come *after* at least one of the relevant words in the ablative.
    E.g. Two years before = duōbus ante annīs.
    E.g. Two years afterwards = duōbus post annīs.

Revision

Write down and learn by heart:

*   The declension of gradus, genū and domus.
*   The regular and irregular imperatives met in this chapter.
*   The declension of ūnus, duo and trēs.
*   The rule for towns, small islands, domus and rūs.
*   The rules for expressions of time.
*   The words in Vocabulary 3.

So you really want to learn Latin...

Exercise 3. 11

Study the information on the left-hand page about expressions of time. Then translate into Latin:

1. For five years
2. Within two years
3. During the night
4. During the third year
5. In the fifth year

6. Five years ago
7. Three hours ago
8. Seven years before
9. Eight years afterwards
10. For many years

Exercise 3. 12

Translate into English:

1. multōs annōs Rōmānī rēgēs timēbant.

2. prīmō annō, Rōmulus urbem regēbat.

3. frātrem multīs ante hōrīs gladiō interfēcerat.

4. "abhinc multōs annōs" inquit "Aenēās ex Āsiā nāvigāvit."

5. multīs post annīs cīvis fortis, nōmine Brūtus, rēgem ex urbe pepulit.

6. rēx Etruscōrum, nōmine Lars Porsenna, Rōmam festīnāvit.

7. Horātius pontem multās hōrās defendēbat nec tamen hostēs superāvit.

8. multīs post annīs, Gallī arcem urbis noctū oppugnāvērunt.

9. mīlitēs Rōmānī dormiēbant sed mediā nocte ānserēs clāmāvērunt.

10. multās hōrās Rōmānī cum hostibus pugnābant.

Exercise 3. 13

Translate into Latin:

1. We will have lived in Italy for five years.

2. The son of the general had attacked the city three years before.

3. Four years later we sailed from Troy to Italy.

4. During the night we heard the soldiers.

5. In the tenth year the citizens drove the old man out of the town.

6. Will you come to the country within two years?

7. After many years the soldiers departed from Rome.

8. Many hours before, the woman had told the story to her daughters.

9. Did you see the moon during the night?

10. The school-master taught the children of the consul for four years.

Using Latin	**Lāpsus linguae**
	Lāpsus linguae = a slip of the tongue.

The Gauls

The Romans, as we know from the adventures of Asterix, had great fun beating up the Gauls. The Gauls were hairy chaps with silly helmets and the odd cauldron full of magic potion.

In the early days of Rome's history, the Gauls were brave enough to roam around Italy, plundering and so on. They began with the city of Clusium (of Lars Porsenna fame) and, in 390 B.C., they turned on the Romans. Defeating them at the Battle of Allia, they marched on Rome itself and boldly entered the city. It was then that their leader, Brennus, is said to have uttered the famous words vae victīs = "woe to the conquered". But there was a problem. Most of the inhabitants, including the soldiers, had withdrawn up on to the Capitoline Hill where they hid in the arx (citadel). Only the oldest senators were unwilling to run away from a bunch of hairy Gauls and eighty of them thus remained in the forum, seated on their ivory chairs in their finest togas. The Gauls entered the forum and at first thought that the old men were statues. But one Gaul went up to one of the "statues", a gentleman by the name of Papirius, and pulled his beard. Papirius bashed him over the head with his staff and was promptly stabbed for his pains. The rest of the old boys were then slaughtered.

For some time the Romans were safe up on their mountain but, one night, a band of Gauls crept up the steepest face of the mountain-side, following the footprints of a brave young Roman, who had himself crept up and down the mountain at that point, attempting to get help for the Romans. The Romans, who never expected the Gauls to scale this side of the mountain, would have been in serious trouble but for a bunch of sacred geese. These geese, sacred to the goddess Juno, heard the Gauls coming and let out the most dreadful cackling. The guards woke up and drove the Gauls down again.

The Romans eventually got rid of the Gauls when an army under a Roman general called Camillus, who had been living in exile, came charging over and defeated the Gauls at the Battle of Gabii. It was not, however, until about three hundred years later that the Romans really got their revenge when, under Julius Caesar, they proceded to carve up Gaul and make it part of the Roman Empire (58–51 B.C.). France, as Gaul is now called, was thus full of Romans and when you next go you must look out for traces of them. Provence, for example, which takes its name from the Latin word prōvincia = "a province", is full of aqueducts, amphitheatres, temples and theatres dating from Roman times, many of them in better condition than anything that can be seen in Italy. For example the amphitheatre and temple at Nîmes, the theatre at Orange, the amphitheatre at Arles and the aqueduct at the Pont du Gard are quite exceptional and have to be seen to be believed.

So you really want to learn Latin...

Exercise 3. 14

Using the information contained in this chapter about the Gauls, answer the following questions in complete sentences:

1. Against whom did the Romans fight at the Battle of Allia, and when?

2. Who was the king of the Gauls at this time?

3. Who won the Battle of Allia and what did the Gauls do after the battle?

4. When the Gauls entered Rome, what had the women and young men done?

5. What did the old men do?

6. What happened to the old men in the forum when the Gauls found them?

7. Why did the Gauls climb up the mountain?

8. What was it that saved the Romans on this occasion?

9. Who eventually came to the rescue of the Romans?

10. When did Gaul become part of the Roman empire and who was responsible for the conquest?

Using Latin	**Vae victīs**
	Vae victīs = woe to the conquered!

CHAPTER 4

The Passive; 5th declension nouns

The Passive

So far, all the verbs you have met have been *active*. The subject of an active verb is the person or thing *doing the verb*.

E.g. the master *is teaching* the pupil.

But when the verb is *passive*, the subject of the verb is the person or thing to whom the verb is "being done".

E.g. the pupil *is being taught* by the master.

Learning the passive tenses is relatively straightforward if you remember the following conversion chart for the verb endings:

Active:	-ō	-s	-t	-mus	-tis	-nt
Passive:	-or	-ris	-tur	-mur	-minī	-ntur

Present passive

The present passive of amō, moneō, regō, audiō and capiō is shown below.

am-or	*I am loved*	mone-or	reg-or	audi-or	capi-or
amā-ris	*You are loved*	monē-ris	reg-eris	audī-ris	cap-eris
amā-tur	*He, she,*	monē-tur	reg-itur	audī-tur	cap-itur
	it is loved				
amā -mur	*We are loved*	monē-mur	reg-imur	audī-mur	cap-imur
amā-minī	*You are loved*	monē-minī	reg-iminī	audī-minī	cap-iminī
ama-ntur	*They are loved*	mone-ntur	reg-untur	audi-untur	capi-untur

Mixed conjugation verbs: a note on the stem

The dead-eyed among you will have noticed that capiō seems to have a certain amount of trouble determining whether its stem is cap- or capi-. As we saw in Book I when we first met capiō, the answer to this knotty problem is that when two vowels come together (e.g. capiō, capiunt, capiam, etc.) the stem is capi- (and the verb is following the 4th conjugation). Where this does not happen (e.g. capis, capit, etc.), the stem is cap- (and it is following the 3rd conjugation).

Passive Infinitives

The present infinitive of a verb may be made passive as shown below. Note how it is generally formed by changing the e of the active infinitive to an ī but, as always, regō and capiō are pigs.

amārī	monērī	regī	audīrī	capī
To be loved	To be warned	To be ruled	To be heard	To be captured

So you really want to learn Latin...

Exercise 4. 1

Study the information on the opposite page about the passive. Then, for each of the following, (a) write out the present tense, active and passive; and (b) give the present infinitive, active and passive:

1. portō
2. teneō
3. iaciō

4. dūcō
5. aperiō
6. frangō

Exercise 4. 2

Translate into English:

1. agricola vidētur.
2. puerī audiuntur.
3. dōnum datur.
4. exercitus dūcitur.
5. servī interficiuntur.

6. mīlitēs ā duce iubentur.
7. iuvenēs ā cōnsule laudantur.
8. vōx puellae audītur.
9. portus dēfenditur.
10. collis ascenditur.

Exercise 4. 3

Translate into Latin:

1. Rome is ruled.
2. You (sing.) are warned.
3. They want to be praised.
4. The slaves are being taught.
5. The tears of the mother are seen.
6. All the soldiers are killed.
7. The city is being defended in vain.
8. The sad women are found in the forum.
9. The bridge is being destroyed.
10. The letter is being sent to your friend.

Exercise 4. 4

More hairy Gauls: translate into English (note that the verbs are in the historic present):

Rōma ā Gallīs oppugnātur. mīlitēs in montem ascendunt sed senēs ā Gallīs inveniuntur. omnēs senēs interficiuntur et Rōmānī terrentur. urbs tamen ab ānseribus sacrīs servātur. Gallī enim dē monte pelluntur et fugere cōguntur.

| *Using Latin* | **Vēnī, vīdī, vīcī**
These famous words of Julius Caesar mean
"I came, I saw, I conquered". |

Future Passive

The future passive tells us what *will be done* to the subject, e.g. I will be loved. Note how the -bō, -bis, -bit endings become -bor, -beris, -bitur, whereas the -am, -ēs, -et endings become -ar, -ēris, -ētur.

amā-bor	monē-bor	reg-ar	audi-ar	capi-ar
amā-beris	monē-beris	reg-ēris*	audi-ēris	capi-ēris
amā-bitur	monē-bitur	reg-ētur	audi-ētur	capi-ētur
amā-bimur	monē-bimur	reg-ēmur	audi-ēmur	capi-ēmur
amā-biminī	monē-biminī	reg-ēminī	audi-ēminī	capi-ēminī
amā-buntur	monē-buntur	reg-entur	audi-entur	capi-entur

* This looks almost identical to the 2nd person singular, present passive (**regeris**); only the pronunciation is different. Typical **regō**, eh?

Imperfect Passive

The imperfect passive tells us what *was being done* to the subject, e.g. I was being loved. Notice how –bam, -bās, -bat becomes –bar, -bāris, -bātur, etc.

amā-bar	monē-bar	reg-ēbar	audi-ēbar	capi-ēbar
amā-bāris	monē-bāris	reg-ēbāris	audi-ēbāris	capi-ēbāris
amā-bātur	monē-bātur	reg-ēbātur	audi-ēbātur	capi-ēbātur
amā-bāmur	monē-bāmur	reg-ēbāmur	audi-ēbāmur	capi-ēbāmur
amā-bāminī	monē-bāminī	reg-ēbāminī	audi-ēbāminī	capi-ēbāminī
amā-bantur	monē-bantur	reg-ēbantur	audi-ēbantur	capi-ēbantur

Agents and instruments

The passive is often followed by an ablative to tell us by whom or what the action of the verb is being done. If this is a *person or animal*, it is an **agent** and must have the preposition ā/ab. If it is a *thing* it is an **instrument** and has no preposition.

E.g. He is loved by the *girl* (agent) = ā puellā amātur.

E.g. He is killed with a *sword* (instrument) = gladiō interficitur.

It is, of course, possible to be attacked by an agent with an instrument, as in the silly picture!

So you really want to learn Latin...

Exercise 4. 5

Study the information on the left-hand page about the future and imperfect tenses. Write out the following:

1. Future passive of superō, superāre   3. Future passive of dūcō, dūcere

2. Imperfect passive of pōnō, pōnere   4. Imperfect passive of iaciō, iacere

Exercise 4. 6

Study the information on the left-hand page about agents and instruments. Then translate into Latin:

1. They will be accused by the judge.

2. The journey will be completed by the soldiers.

3. Ambassadors will be sent by the general.

4. The fortunate slaves will not be killed by the sword.

5. The legion is being sent to Rome.

6. She was being warned by the master.

7. They will be thrown into the river by the farmer.

8. The camp of the enemy was being attacked with arrows.

9. The letter was being written with great care[1].

10. The children[2] of the master will be terrified by the storm.

N.B. 1. magnā cum cūrā. The manner in which something happens or is done is either expressed by an ablative with an adjective in agreement; or by using the preposition cum + ablative (with or without an adjective).

2. The Latin for "children", when it means someone's "offspring" or "sons and/or daughters", is līberī, -ōrum, m.pl. This word is not used to mean "children" in the sense of, simply, "young boys and girls".

Exercise 4. 7

Translate into English: *The story of Titus Manlius, 362 B.C.*

ōlim pater Rōmānus, nōmine Lūcius Mānlius, ā cīvibus accūsābātur. Lūcius enim fīlium in agrōs mīserat quod is stultus erat. sed puer, Titus Mānlius, nōn erat īrātus et patrem superbum amābat. tandem cīvēs senem in forum vocāvērunt. Titus tamen patrem adiuvāre cupiēbat. domum igitur tribūnī intrāvit et "tē interficiam" inquit "quod patrem meum accūsāvistī". tribūnus igitur senem līberāvit et Titus Mānlius ab omnibus laudābātur.

tribūnus, -ī, m. = tribune (a sort of judge in Rome).

	Ars longa, vīta brevis
Using Latin	The motto of all true artists, this famous phrase means "Art (is) long (but) life (is) short".

5th declension nouns: rēs and diēs

Now for some sad news: there is only one more declension to learn. No more flicking to the back to find out how many more declensions. This is the last one. Nouns of the 5th declension decline like rēs or diēs. They are all feminine except diēs = "day" and merīdiēs = "noon" which are masculine (actually even diēs is feminine when it refers to an *appointed* day). N.B. Nouns in –iēs (e.g. diēs) have a long –ē in the genitive and dative singular (e.g. diēī).

	rēs, reī, f. = thing, affair		diēs, diēī, m. = day	
	Singular	**Plural**	**Singular**	**Plural**
Nominative	r-ēs	r-ēs	di-ēs	di-ēs
Vocative	r-ēs	r-ēs	di-ēs	di-ēs
Accusative	r-em	r-ēs	di-em	di-ēs
Genitive	r-eī	r-ērum	di-ēī	di-ērum
Dative	r-eī	r-ēbus	di-ēī	di-ēbus
Ablative	r-ē	r-ēbus	di-ē	di-ēbus

Vocabulary 4

Nouns

animus, animī, m.	mind, spirit
cūra, cūrae, f.	care
diēs, diēī, m.	day
fortūna, -ae, f.	fortune
forum, forī, n.	forum
iūdex, iūdicis, c.	judge
lēgātus, lēgātī, m.	ambassador
legiō, legiōnis, f.	legion
lēx, lēgis, f.	law
līberī, līberōrum, m. pl.	offspring, sons and daughters
rēs, reī, f.	thing, affair

Preposition

propter + acc.	on account of

Verbs

accūsō, -āre, -āvī, -ātum	I accuse
cōnficiō, -ere, cōnfēcī, cōnfectum	I complete
dēspērō, -āre, -āvī, -ātum	I despair
līberō, -āre, -āvī, -ātum	I free
lūdō, -ere, lūsī, lūsum	I play

Adjectives

dīligēns, dīligentis	careful, diligent
fēlīx, fēlīcis	fortunate, happy, favourable
līber, lībera, līberum	free

Revision

Write down and learn by heart:
* The present, future and imperfect passive endings.
* The passive infinitives.
* The rule about agents and instruments.
* The nouns rēs and diēs.
* The words in Vocabulary 4.

So you really want to learn Latin...

Exercise 4. 8
Study the information on the left-hand page about 5th declension nouns. Then translate into Latin:

1. He remained in the city for five days.
2. They will attack Rome within three days.
3. The ambassador completed the affair with great care.
4. We will conduct the affairs of the city for one year.
5. They sailed to the small island seven days ago.

Exercise 4. 9
Translate into English: *Manlius Torquatus, 361 B.C.*

Gallī Rōmam oppugnāre cupiēbant. exercitus autem Rōmānus cum Gallīs ab imperātōre dūcēbātur. inter mīlitēs erat Titus Mānlius. Gallī Rōmānōs nōn superāverant et fessī erant. "nōnne ūnus Rōmānus" inquit mīles Gallus "cum ūnō Gallō pugnābit?" Rōmānī diū Gallum spectābant. tandem Titus Mānlius "egŏ" inquit "cum eō Gallō pugnābō."

in pugnā Titus Mānlius Gallum ingentem interfēcit et <u>torquem</u> eius cēpit. ā Rōmānīs laudābātur et propter torquem Torquātus appellābātur.

torquis, -is, c. = necklace

Exercise 4. 10
Study the words in Vocabulary 4. From which Latin words are the following derived? Translate the Latin word and explain the meaning of the English one.

1. Animated
2. Felicitous
3. Desperate
4. Diligent
5. Fortunate
6. Liberate
7. Accusation
8. Judicious
9. Legal
10. Civil

Exercise 4. 11
Revision. Translate, without looking up:

1. cecidit
2. appellant
3. ascendērunt
4. post carmen
5. tēcum
6. erit
7. sunt
8. esse
9. fac!
10. cūr?

Using Latin

Bona fidēs
Bona fidēs = "good faith". For example: "the Police checked his bona fidēs and were satisfied".

Rome: home and away

The history of Rome at this stage is dominated by two major struggles. At home there was the ongoing class war between the patricians and the plebeians. The plebeians wanted more land, less tax and protection from the oppression of patrician magistrates (thus the story of Verginia in Chapter 2). They also wanted to be allowed to hold political office in the city. The patricians, on the other hand, wanted to keep the plebeians in the gutter. All of this dragged on for a very long time and ended in compromise c. 376 B.C. with the passing of some laws (the Licinian Laws) which seemed to keep everybody happy.

Much more interesting was the other major struggle, that of Rome against the rest of Italy. Keen to hold her own in the world, Rome had first to start by controlling Italy and it wasn't quite as easy as it seemed. We have seen the trouble she had at the hands of the hairy Gauls. The Roman defeat at the Battle of Allia in 387 had seriously damaged her reputation with her neighbours and in 340 the Latins and the Campanians revolted against Rome. They thought that half of the Roman senate should be made up of Latins (rather than Romans) and that one of the consuls should be a Latin. The Romans did not agree and war was declared. The two consuls at the time were Manlius Torquatus and a chap called Publius Decius. After these two had led their armies to meet the enemy near Capua a very strange thing happened. In the night, both consuls had the same dream. They dreamt that a giant had come to them and said that the army whose general sacrificed himself to the gods of the underworld would be victorious in the battle.

Manlius Torquatus briefed the army the next day, giving strict instructions that nobody should attack the enemy until ordered to do so. This would have been fine except that some arrogant Latin horseman, fed up with waiting for the battle to start, jeered at the Romans, claiming they were cowards. Manlius Torquatus's son, who happened to be within hearing range of this insult, was unimpressed and rode out to sort things out with the Latin. Having killed him, he rode back to his own side where he was promptly killed by his father for disobeying orders. The soldiers were, naturally enough, somewhat shocked by this harsh treatment, but none of them ever disobeyed an order again!

When the battle did eventually take place, the enemy were pushing the Romans back on the left flank. Remembering the words of the giant in the dream, Publius Decius said his final prayers and charged out into the midst of the enemy where he was promptly turned into mincemeat. However it set a jolly good example to his men and in an hour or so they had won the battle.

So you really want to learn Latin...

Exercise 4. 12

Study the information opposite about Rome, home and away, and then answer the following questions in complete sentences:

1. In the class war which dominated the history of this period, what did the plebeians want which the patricians were unwilling to let them have?

2. How and when was this conflict resolved?

3. What effect had the Romans' defeat at Allia had upon the rest of Italy?

4. Who was it that revolted against Rome in 340 B.C.?

5. What were the demands of these rebels?

6. Who were the two Roman consuls at this time and what did they do?

7. Describe the dream which the two consuls had.

8. Describe what happened when Manlius Torquatus's son responded to a challenge from an Italian horseman.

9. Why do you think Manlius Torquatus chose to kill his son and what effect did this have on discipline in the army?

10. Describe how the consuls' dream eventually led to the success of the Romans in the battle against the Latins.

Using Latin	**Aegrōtat**
	An aegrōtat degree is one awarded to a student who is too ill to take his/her exams. Aegrōtat = "he/she is ill".

CHAPTER 5
The perfect, future perfect and pluperfect passive

Perfect passive
The perfect passive tells us what *has been done* to the subject, e.g. "I have been loved". It is formed by taking a glorious little chap, the Perfect (or Past) Participle Passive (the P.P.P. to his friends), and combining it with the verb "to be". The P.P.P. of a verb means "having been loved" etc. and is formed from the *supine stem*, found in the 4th principal part. All you have to do is change the -um to -us.

amāt-us, -a, -um	sum	I have been loved
amāt-us -a, -um	es	You (sing.) have been loved
amāt-us, -a, -um	est	He, she, it has been loved
amāt-ī, -ae, -a	sumus	We have been loved
amāt-ī, -ae, -a	estis	You (pl.) have been loved
amāt-ī, -ae, -a	sunt	They have been loved

Note that the P.P.P. is an adjective, declining like bonus. If the subject is masculine and singular, the ending is –us. But if it is feminine, this becomes –a, and so on.

To form the perfect passive
The more musical among you now have the opportunity to sing a little song, with loads of *tiddly tums* thrown in. The tune is very much an acquired taste, but here we go:

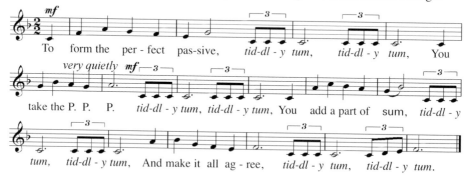

This song will probably drive you mad pretty quickly, but it does work and, after all, what's a bit of insanity between friends?

P.s. Don't forget to make the P.P.P. agree with the subject!

Thus: He has been loved (or was loved) = amātus est
      She has been loved (or was loved) = amāta est
      The boys have been loved (or were loved) = puerī amātī sunt
      The girls have been loved (or were loved) = puellae amātae sunt

So you really want to learn Latin...

Exercise 5. 1

Study the information on the opposite page about the perfect passive. Write out the perfect passive of:

1. moneō   2. regō   3. audiō   4. capiō

Exercise 5. 2

Translate into English. Note how the P.P.P. changes to agree with the subject. E.g. in sentence 1, missus becomes missae to agree with the subject (nāvēs, which is feminine plural).

1. paucae nāvēs ad īnsulam <u>multīs cum legiōnibus</u>* missae sunt.

2. mīles ā lēgātō novō accūsātus est.

3. paucās noctēs urbs ab hostibus oppugnābātur.

4. puella per portās urbis ducta est.

5. victōria populō Rōmānō nūntiāta est.

6. "nostrī" inquit "ā Gallīs numquam superābuntur."

7. nunc pānis in oppidum ā līberīs cōnsulis portātur.

8. nōmen lēgātī novī sciēbāmus.

9. "auxilium" inquiunt "ā cōpiīs novīs datum est."

10. multae fābulae nārrātae sunt.

* multīs cum legiōnibus is more stylish Latin than cum multīs legiōnibus. The preposition likes to precede the noun, not the adjective. Therefore, as multus comes before its noun, rather than after it, the preposition has to dive in between it and the legions.

Exercise 5. 3

Translate into Latin, remembering to make the P.P.P. agree with the subject:

1. The boy has been called.

2. The girl has been called.

3. The war has been prepared.

4. The boys have been taught.

5. The girls have been watched.

6. The wars have been waged.

7. The footsoldiers have been seen by the enemy.

8. The city was destroyed by a few slaves.

9. The Romans were terrified by the new king.

10. Part of the story was told by your teacher.

Using Latin	**Ad īnfīnītum** If someone talks ad īnfīnītum, they go on and on for ever. Īnfīnītus = unlimited.

Future perfect passive

The future perfect passive tells us what *shall* or *will have been done* to the subject. It is formed in the same way as the perfect, except that the *future* tense of sum is added.

amāt-us, -a, -um	erō	I shall/will have been loved
amāt-us, -a, -um	eris	You (sing.) will have been loved
amāt-us, -a, -um	erit	He, she, it will have been loved
amāt-ī, -ae, -a	erimus	We shall/will have been loved
amāt-ī, -ae, -a	eritis	You (pl.) will have been loved
amāt-ī, -ae, -a	erunt	They will have been loved

Pluperfect passive

The pluperfect passive tells us what *had been done* to the subject. This time it is the imperfect of sum that we add.

amāt-us, -a, -um	eram	I had been loved
amāt-us, -a, -um	erās	You (sing.) had been loved
amāt-us, -a, -um	erat	He, she, it had been loved
amāt-ī, -ae, -a	erāmus	We had been loved
amāt-ī, -ae, -a	erātis	You (pl.) had been loved
amāt-ī, -ae, -a	erant	They had been loved

Vocabulary 5

Nouns

nāvis, nāvis, f.	ship
nihil	nothing
nox, noctis, f.	night
ōrātiō, ōrātiōnis, f.	speech
pānis, pānis, m.	bread
pars, partis, f.	part
pedes, peditis, m.	foot-soldier
pēs, pedis, m.	foot
populus, populī, m.	people
porta, -ae, f.	gate

Adjectives

paucī, -ae, -a	few
valēns, valentis [1]	strong
validus, -a, -um	strong

Verbs

nesciō[2], nescīre, nescīvī, nescītum	I do not know
nūntiō, -āre, -āvī, -ātum	I announce, report
petō, petere, petīvī, petītum	I seek
putō[2], -āre, -āvī, -ātum	I think
sciō[2], scīre, scīvī, scītum	I know

Adverbs

numquam	never
nunc	now
tum	then, next
tunc	then

Conjunction

nam	for

N.B. 1. Valēns is considered to be a better word to use for "strong" than validus.
2. The final –o of sciō, nesciō and putō is often found short in verse.

So you really want to learn Latin...

Exercise 5. 4
Read the information on the opposite page about the future perfect and pluperfect passive. Then translate into Latin:

1. She will have been warned.
2. You (sing.) will have been terrified.
3. The gift will have been given to the small boy.
4. The enemy will have been defeated by the Romans.
5. The consuls will have been chosen already.
6. I had been forced to flee seven days before.
7. She had been killed five years before.
8. Why had you not been warned?
9. The king had been driven out of the city during the night.
10. The bridge had been destroyed after many hours.

Exercise 5. 5
Translate into English:

1. puerī puellaeque ā magistrō territī erant.
2. omnēs servī in forum pulsī erant.
3. puella misera in arce quīnque diēs manēre coācta erat.
4. nōnne barbarī ē patriā mox pulsī erunt?
5. fīlius cōnsulis sub mēnsā vīsus erat.

Exercise 5. 6
Translate into Latin:

A Roman citizen had been sent into the fields because his father did not love him. The people of Rome were angry and accused the citizen. The boy, however, wanted to save the old man. For the father was loved by the son. Therefore the boy came to the house of the tribune and said "I had been sent into the fields but I love my father and want to save him."

Using Latin	**Prō tem.** Prō tem. is short for prō tempore = "for the time", i.e. temporarily.

Fancy tricks with the P.P.P.

We have seen how the perfect, future perfect and pluperfect passive tenses are formed by combining a verb's Past Participle Passive with a tense of the verb sum. Thus the perfect passive form amātus est really means "he is" (est) "having been loved" (amātus). We don't translate it like this, of course, but that is what it means.

But because the tense is formed by combining these two words, we are able to play around with the word order. Thus, if we are feeling particularly stylish, instead of writing amātus est we write est amātus.

Another thing we can do, when we are really trying to impress our friends and relations, is leave out the part of sum altogether. You have to be careful with this one, but if a sentence has more than one verb in, let us say, the perfect passive, and the subject of each one is the same, then you can leave out the sum bit from one of the verbs.

E.g. mīlitēs superātī ~~sunt~~ et fugere coāctī sunt =
the soldiers were overcome and ~~were~~ forced to flee.

You will notice that we do this ourselves in English the whole time, only with English it would always be the second verb that we shorten, not the first.

E.g. The soldiers were overcome and ~~were~~ forced to flee.

In Book III we will show you how to be even more stylish, by leaving out the "and" as well as the part of sum. For those of you who can't wait, try to work out what this means: mīlitēs superātī ~~sunt et~~ fugere coāctī sunt.

If you translate the P.P.P. (superātī) literally (i.e. "having been overcome"), you should be able to cope.

Revision

Make sure you know by heart:

* The six tenses, active and passive of all your verbs (amō, moneō, regō, audiō and capiō).

* The present infinitives, active and passive.

* Regular nouns of the five declensions (mēnsa; annus, bellum, puer, magister; rēx, opus, cīvis, cubīle; gradus, genū; rēs).

* Irregular nouns: fīlius, deus, vir, domus.

* Egŏ, tū, nōs, vōs; is, ea, id.

* Numerals 1–20 and 1st–10th.

* Declension of ūnus, duo and trēs.

* Vocabularies 1–5 in this book and 1–10 in Book I.

So you really want to learn Latin...

Exercise 5. 7
Read the information on the left-hand page about the P.P.P. Then translate into English:
Filial disobedience, 340 B.C.

Mānlius Torquātus cōnsul erat cum Pūbliō Deciō. bellum autem cum Latīnīs Rōmānī gerēbant. ōlim Mānlius mīlitēs vocāvit et "cum hostibus" inquit "pugnāre nōn cupiō." sed eques Latīnus magnā vōce clāmāvit "Rōmānī" inquit "pugnāre nōn cupiunt; Rōmānī Latīnōs timent." fīlius autem Mānliī Torquātī verba eius audīvit. gladium igitur cēpit et in hostēs cucurrit. eques Latīnus ā Rōmānō fortī vulnerātus et interfectus est.

pater, tamen, īrātus erat. "nōnne" inquit "verba mea ā tē audīta sunt? cūr cum hostibus pugnāvistī?" tum fīlius miser ā patre captus et gladiō est interfectus.

Exercise 5. 8
Translate into Latin:

In that year the two consuls, Manlius Torquatus and Publius Decius, had a dream. The god said to them "a general will be killed but his army will overcome the enemy". Therefore, in the battle, because the Romans were being forced by the Latins to flee, Publius Decius ran into the enemy. "I will save my fatherland" he said. The consul was killed but the Romans saw his death and ran into the forces of the enemy. The Latins were overcome and were forced to flee.

Exercise 5. 9
Translate into English: *The Caudine Forks, 321 B.C.*

dum cōpiae Rōmānae Ītaliam superant, tria bella cum Samnītibus gessērunt. bellō autem secundō dux Samnītium, nōmine Gāius Pontius, castra prope Caudium posuit. tum cōnsilium ita cēpit. decem peditēs in agrīs ambulāre iussit. peditēs ā Rōmānīs captī sunt. "exercitus Samnītium" inquiunt peditēs "ad urbem Lūceriam iam discessit." Rōmānī Lūceriam festīnāvērunt quod urbem servāre cupiēbant.

duae viae ad urbem <u>ferēbant</u>. erat prope mare via longa, per montēs via brevis. Rōmānī per montēs iter faciēbant et īn <u>saltū</u> <u>angustō</u>, nōmine <u>Furculīs</u> Caudīnīs, ā Latīnīs superātī sunt. Rōmānī ā Latīnīs pācem petere sunt coāctī et omnēs mīlitēs sub <u>iugum</u> missī sunt.*

ferō = I lead (of a road); saltus, -ūs, m. = pass; angustus, -a, -um = narrow; furcula, -ae, f. = fork; iugum, -ī, n. = yoke

*To send an enemy under the yoke (sub iugum mittere) was a traditional form of humiliation.

Using Latin

Per annum
Per annum = through/during a year.

Roman education

Under the republic, Roman boys were educated by their fathers, girls (mainly) by their mothers. There were two main aspects to the education the boys received: on the one hand they learnt how to farm, following their fathers into the fields and learning by observation. On the other hand they studied the Twelve Tables and the mōs maiōrum (= the custom of their ancestors). As we have seen, the Twelve Tables contained all the laws which affected Roman citizens (see the story of Verginia, Chapter 2) and had to be learnt by heart. The mōs maiōrum was a body of stories, repeated over the generations, which gave the young Roman an example of how to live. Respect for the father of the house (pater familiās) was paramount. Beyond this, the aim of the Roman citizen was to live a life marked by pietās (respect for the gods, one's fatherland and one's parents) and gravitās (seriousness). It was felt that by studying the actions of his ancestors he could be brought to achieve this aim. That is why so much attention was given to the stories of daring such as that of Horatius on the bridge, or of obedience and loyalty such as that of Titus Manlius.

At the age of about seven, boys and some girls were sent to school. The first school, which might be in a room above a shop or even just in a colonnade near the forum, was kept by a badly-paid and often bad-tempered teacher called the litterātor or lūdī magister. His job was to teach the pupils to read and write. At the age of eleven or twelve pupils moved on to the grammaticus, who taught grammar and literature. This often involved learning large chunks of Greek and Latin poetry by heart. Some boys would then go to a rhētōr to learn the art of rhetoric or public speaking. Finally, the boys finished off their education by a spell in the army, where they put into practice all the qualities of courage and virtue which they had learnt through the stories of their ancestors.

So teachers then, much as today, were bad-tempered, badly-paid thugs. But it wasn't always the teachers who were the violent ones. The story is told of how, when Camillus (the general who saved Rome from the Gauls) was besieging the Etruscan town of Falerii c. 396 B.C., a school-master led his class of boys out of the town and into the Roman camp. He knew that the boys were all sons of rich citizens and thought that, if they fell into the hands of the Roman army, their parents would be willing to pay a huge ransom to get them back, part of which he would keep for himself. Camillus, however, was unimpressed by the school master's treachery and, giving the boys rods, ordered them to beat the master all the way back to the town.

So you really want to learn Latin...

Exercise 5. 10

Read the information on the left-hand page about Roman education. Then answer the following questions in complete sentences:

1. What were the two main aspects of Roman education for boys under the republic?

2. What were the Twelve Tables?

3. Who was the pater familiās?

4. What was pietās? Which English word is derived from pietās?

5. What was gravitās? Which English word is derived from gravitās?

6. How were young Romans encouraged to achieve these two qualities?

7. At what age did children go to school?

8. Which type of teacher taught children to read and write?

9. Which type of teacher taught them grammar and literature?

10. Which type of teacher taught the art of rhetoric, and what was rhetoric?

Using Latin

Ars artis grātiā
Ars artis grātiā = art for the sake of art.

CHAPTER 6
The comparison of adjectives; Roman dates

Regular comparison of adjectives

Adjectives may be *compared* in three degrees: positive, comparative and superlative. The positive is the normal form of the adjective. The *comparative* is formed by adding -ior (a small donkey?) to the stem of the adjective. The *superlative* is formed by adding -issimus to the stem of the adjective.

Positive	Comparative	Superlative
longus	long-ior	long-issimus
Long	Longer, more long	Longest, most long, very long
trīstis	trīst-ior	trīst-issimus
Sad	Sadder, more sad	Saddest, most sad, very sad

Declension of comparative and superlative adjectives

Irrespective of what declension the adjective is to start with, comparatives decline like melior, melius = "better", and superlatives decline like bonus, -a, -um.

melior, melius = better		
	M	**F**	**N**
Nom.	melior	melior	melius
Voc.	melior	melior	melius
Acc.	meliōr-em	meliōr-em	melius
Gen.	meliōr-is	meliōr-is	meliōr-is
Dat.	meliōr-ī	meliōr-ī	meliōr-ī
Abl.	meliōr-e	meliōr-e	meliōr-e
Nom.	meliōr-ēs	meliōr-ēs	meliōr-a
Voc.	meliōr-ēs	meliōr-ēs	meliōr-a
Acc.	meliōr-ēs	meliōr-ēs	meliōr-a
Gen.	meliōr-um	meliōr-um	meliōr-um
Dat.	meliōr-ibus	meliōr-ibus	meliōr-ibus
Abl.	meliōr-ibus	meliōr-ibus	meliōr-ibus

Comparing nouns

1. Two nouns being compared using quam = "than" must be in the same case:
   E.g. puella trīstior est quam puer = the girl is sadder than the boy.
2. Alternatively, if two persons or things are **directly compared**, an ablative of comparison may be used, with the second noun being put in the ablative (without quam). E.g. puella trīstior est puerō = the girl is sadder than the boy.

   In this example the girl is being directly compared with the boy. However, in a sentence such as "Marcus has a better horse than Brutus (has)", we could not use an ablative of comparison because Marcus's horse is not better than Brutus, it is better than Brutus's *horse*, thus Mārcus meliōrem equum habet quam Brūtus.

So you really want to learn Latin...

Exercise 6. 1

Read the information on the opposite page about the comparison of adjectives. Note that the -ior and -issimus are added to the **stem** of the adjective. Then give the comparative and superlative of:

1. dūrus, -a, -um
2. laetus, -a, -um
3. cārus, -a, -um
4. īrātus, -a, -um
5. altus, -a, -um

6. ingēns, ingentis
7. dīligēns, dīligentis
8. fortis, forte
9. fēlīx, fēlīcis
10. audāx, audācis

Exercise 6. 2

Study the information on the opposite page about the declension of comparative and superlative adjectives. Then translate into Latin:

1. Of the sadder girl
2. The braver kings (nom.)
3. The longer wars (nom.)
4. The very angry master (nom.)
5. Of the most happy woman

6. For the most fortunate general
7. With the boldest soldiers
8. On the higher mountain
9. Near the deeper river
10. O most happy farmers!

Exercise 6. 3

Read the information on the opposite page about comparing nouns. Then translate into Latin:

1. The king was braver than the consul.
2. The Romans waged a very long war.
3. The Roman soldiers are bolder than the barbarians.
4. Our mother is more sad than your father.
5. Send a longer letter to me!
6. The Romans were overcome by bolder footsoldiers.
7. We have a braver leader than you (i.e. than you have).
8. The mountains are higher than the city.

Exercise 6. 4

Translate into English:

ōlim puer Rōmānus ā patre īrātissimō docēbātur. puer multa dē fortibus Rōmānīs didicit sed perīcula bellī semper timēbat. itaque pater puerum miserum in bellum mīsit. inter mīlitēs fortissimōs diū pugnābat et itinera longissima saepe faciēbat. tandem puer domum revēnit et patrem vīdit. "ōlim tē nōn amābam" inquit "sed nunc audācior sum quam omnēs mīlitēs. cīvis Rōmānus fēlīcissimus sum. multās grātiās tibī agō."

Using Latin	**Carpe diem** A useful piece of advice made famous by the Roman poet, Horace, carpe diem = seize the day!

Adjectives in -er and -ilis
Adjectives in -er change -er to -errimus instead of -issimus to form their superlative:

| Tender | tener | tenerior | tenerrimus |
| Beautiful | pulcher | pulchrior | pulcherrimus |

Six adjectives in -ilis go -illimus instead of -issimus:

Easy	facilis	facilior	facillimus
Difficult	difficilis	difficilior	difficillimus
Similar	similis	similior	simillimus

Thus also gracilis = slender; humilis = lowly; dissimilis = dissimilar.

Irregular comparison
The following common adjectives are irregular in comparison:

Good	bonus	melior	optimus
Bad	malus	peior	pessimus
Big	magnus	maior	maximus
Small	parvus	minor	minimus
Much, many	multus	plūs*	plūrimus

*Plūs, plūris is used in the singular as a neuter noun followed by a genitive.
E.g. He wants more money = plūs pecūniae cupit.
In the plural it is used as an adjective, declining as follows:
Masc. and Fem.: plūrēs, plūrēs, plūrēs, plūrium, plūribus, plūribus
Neut.: plūra, plūra, plūra, plūrium, plūribus, plūribus
E.g. He wants more forces = plūrēs cōpiās cupit.

Vocabulary 6
Nouns
dolor, dolōris, m.	pain
epistola, -ae, f.	letter
lūdus, lūdī, m.	school
proelium, proeliī, n.	battle
signum, signī, n.	signal, sign
socius, sociī, m.	ally
taberna, -ae, f.	inn

Adjective
| tālis, tāle | such |

Conjunctions
postquam	after
quam	than
quamquam	although
sī	if

Verbs
ostendō, -ere, ostendī, ostēnsum/ostentum	I show
pāreō, pārēre, pāruī, pāritum + dat.	I obey
persuādeō, -ēre, persuāsī, persuāsum + dat.	I persuade
relinquō, relinquere, relīquī, relictum	I leave, abandon
respondeō, -ēre, respondī, respōnsum	I reply

Adverbs
paene	almost
prīmō / prīmum	at first
statim	immediately

So you really want to learn Latin...

Exercise 6. 5

Read the information on the opposite page about adjectives in –er and –ilis and irregular comparison. Give the comparative and superlative of:

1. līber, lībera, līberum
2. miser, misera, miserum
3. parvus, -a, -um
4. pulcher, pulchra, pulchrum
5. malus, -a, -um
6. magnus, -a, -um

Exercise 6. 6

Give the Latin for:

1. Of the biggest city
2. In the deepest river
3. The most beautiful songs (acc.)
4. The worst dangers (nom.)
5. For the bolder soldiers
6. The most difficult work (acc.)
7. On a very easy journey
8. On the easier journeys
9. After the longest war
10. Before the greatest battle

Exercise 6. 7

Study the words in Vocabulary 6 and the irregular comparisons on the left-hand page. Translate and then give an English word derived from:

1. optimus
2. pessimus
3. minimus
4. maximus
5. ostendit
6. signum
7. sociōrum
8. responderant
9. epistola
10. relīquit

Exercise 6. 8

Translate into English: *The Battle of Heraclea, 280 B.C.*

nunc Rōma erat urbs maxima Ītaliae et multī ā Rōmānīs auxilium petēbant. cīvēs tamen Tarentī Rōmānōs nōn amābant et auxilium ā Graecīs petīvērunt. erat autem in Graeciā rēx nōmine Pyrrhus. is multās terrās regere cupiēbat. postquam* cīvēs Tarentī auxilium petīvērunt, Pyrrhus plūrimīs cum mīlitibus in Ītaliam vēnit. Rōmānōs superāvit prope Hēraclēam, sed plūrimī mīlitēs Graecī interfectī sunt.

post proelium "sī" inquit rēx "tālem victōriam iterum habuerō**, sine exercitū domum iter faciam."

Tarentum, -ī, n. = Tarentum

* N.B. postquam is a conjunction and is normally followed by a perfect tense in Latin which is often translated by a pluperfect in English. E.g. postquam petīvit = after he *had* sought.
** Note how Latin uses future perfects where we tend to use a present tense in English. Thus sī victōriam habuerō = "if I will have won a victory", i.e. "if I win a victory".

Using Latin

Maximum
The word *maximum* means "greatest", from the Latin maximus.

Ordinals up to 20th

We have already learnt ordinals from 1st to 10th. In a moment we are going to down tools for a bit and learn about Roman dates. Before doing so, however, we need to learn the ordinals up to 20th.

1st	prīmus	11th	ūndecimus
2nd	secundus	12th	duodecimus
3rd	tertius	13th	tertius decimus
4th	quārtus	14th	quārtus decimus
5th	quīntus	15th	quīntus decimus
6th	sextus	16th	sextus decimus
7th	septimus	17th	septimus decimus
8th	octāvus	18th	duodēvīcēsimus*
9th	nōnus	19th	ūndēvīcēsimus*
10th	decimus	20th	vīcēsimus*

* or vīcēnsimus

Roman dates

There were three key dates in the Roman month: the Kalends, the Nones and the Ides. All other dates were calculated as being so many days before the next key date, for example "on the fourth day before the Ides of March". The Kalends were on the first of the month, the Nones normally on the 5th and the Ides usually on the 13th; but:

In March, July, October and May,
The Nones and Ides use a different day.
In March, July, October and May,
The 7th teams up with the 15th day.

The months

The Roman months were, after a few renaming sessions to honour Julius Caesar and Augustus Caesar, the same as ours: Iānuārius, Februārius, Mārtius, Aprīlis, Maius, Iūnius, Iūlius, Augustus, September, Octōber, November, December. Their year began in March, though, which is why September was their *seventh* month, October was their *eighth* month, and so on.

The months are adjectives, those in –us going like bonus, those in –er going like ācer and Aprīlis going like trīstis.

To calculate a Roman date:

(a) For dates before the Nones and Ides: take the date you want away from the date of the Nones or Ides (whichever comes next) and add 1.
E.g. 3rd January:
Next key date is the Nones, on the 5th.
Thus 5th – 3rd = 2nd, + 1 = 3rd.
Answer: third day before the Nones of January = ante diem tertium Nōnās Iānuāriās.

So you really want to learn Latin...

(b) For dates before the Kalends: take the date you want away from the number of days in the month, and add 2.
E.g. 21st January:
31 (days in January) – 21 = 10, + 2 = 12.
Answer: twelfth day before the Kalends of February =
ante diem duodecimum Kalendās Februāriās.

(c) The day before a key date is given as prīdiē, e.g. prīdiē Kalendās Februāriās = the day before the Kalends of February.

Date formats
1. The key dates are written in the ablative (for time "when"). Kalendae and Nōnae are 1st declension feminine plural nouns, Īdūs is a 4th declension feminine plural noun. Thus Kalendīs Iānuāriīs = *on* the Kalends of January. Nōnīs Iānuāriīs = *on* the Nones of January. Īdibus Iānuāriīs = *on* the Ides of January.
2. The ante diem dates are written in the accusative, with the actual date being expressed as so many days ante the next key date. With ante governing the accusative, the key date would have been accusative, e.g. ante Kalendās. The rest of the phrase was then written between the ante and the key date, and the whole lot was rammed into the accusative case. E.g. ante diem duodecimum Kalendās Februāriās. Easy, eh?
3. Roman dates were abbreviated (thank goodness), with a.d. standing for ante diem and a numeral being used for the ordinal.
E.g. ante diem duodecimum Kalendās Februāriās would be abbreviated to a.d. XII Kal. Feb.

Apart from all of the above, Roman dates were laughably easy to use.

Exercise 6. 9
Study the information about Roman dates. Now write *in full* in Latin:
1. March 13th
2. January 4th
3. June 21st
4. April 1st
5. December 25th
6. October 15th
7. November 5th
8. July 30th
9. February 4th
10. Your birthday

Exercise 6. 10
What are the following dates?
1. ante diem IV Kalendās Aprīlēs
2. prīdiē Nōnās Iūliās
3. ante diem X Kalendās Decembrēs
4. Nōnīs Augustīs
5. Īdibus Iūniīs
6. ante diem III Nōnas Novembrēs
7. ante diem IV Īdūs Februāriās
8. Kalendīs Octōbribus
9. Īdibus Mārtiīs
10. ante diem XIV Kalendās Maiās

Alma māter
Using Latin
Pupils sometimes describe their school or university as their alma māter = "nurturing mother".

Page 54

Rome's domination of Italy

As we have seen, Rome was keen to increase her grip on central and southern Italy and this brought her into conflict with the Samnites, a tough bunch of mountain-dwellers who lived in the south of Italy. In the 1st Samnite War (343-341) Rome helped the city of Capua to drive the Samnites out of Campania. In the 2nd Samnite War (327-304), apart from the "minor mishap" at the Caudine Forks, which we read about in Exercise 5. 9, things went pretty well and the Samnites sued for peace in 304 B.C. Finally, in the 3rd Samnite War (298-290), the Romans managed to polish off the job. This left her pretty much in control of Italy.

However, not everybody liked this situation and in around 280 B.C. the people of Tarentum appealed to the Greek King Pyrrhus of Epirus for help. Pyrrhus was keen to achieve some star status, thinking as he did that he was descended from the Greek hero Achilles, and he set off for Italy at the head of a huge army which included twenty elephants. When he arrived, having lost part of his army in a storm, he set up camp near Heraclea and waited for the Romans. In the battle which followed the Romans were defeated but so many of Pyrrhus's men were killed that he said that, if he won any more victories like that one, he would be forced to return to Greece alone.

The Romans then sent ambassadors to Pyrrhus to negotiate for the return of prisoners. The chief ambassador was an impoverished Roman called Fabricius, who greatly impressed Pyrrhus by refusing a bribe which would have made him extremely rich. Determined to win Fabricius over, the next day, Pyrrhus tried to frighten him by hiding one of his elephants behind a curtain and then suddenly drawing the curtain to reveal the beast. Fabricius had never seen an elephant before but he remained cool and told Pyrrhus that he could be moved neither by money nor by fear of elephants.

The next year Fabricius displayed great character again when he received a letter from Pyrrhus's doctor, offering to poison the king in return for a sum of money. Fabricius immediately wrote to Pyrrhus, informing him of the treachery of his doctor and suggesting that he find himself a new one!

Soon after this the Romans were again defeated at the Battle of Asculum. This time Pyrrhus lost so many men that he said "If we defeat the Romans once more, we shall be completely destroyed!" This is the origin of the expression "a Pyrrhic victory", which refers to a victory which is only won at great cost to the victor.

Revision

Write down and learn by heart:

* The rules for the regular comparison of adjectives.
* The declension of melior.
* The irregular comparison of bonus, malus, magnus, parvus and multus.
* The words in Vocabulary 6.

So you really want to learn Latin...

Exercise 6. 11

Study the information on the left-hand page about Rome's domination of Italy and then answer the following questions in complete sentences:

1. What were the dates of the 1st, 2nd and 3rd Samnite Wars?

2. What was the result of the Samnite wars?

3. Why did the people of Tarentum appeal to King Pyrrhus?

4. Who was King Pyrrhus?

5. What was the outcome of the Battle of Heraclea?

6. Why was Fabricius sent to Pyrrhus?

7. Why did Pyrrhus consider that Fabricius would probably be easy to bribe?

8. What did Pyrrhus do when he had failed to bribe Fabricius?

9. What was Fabricius's response to this?

10. How did Fabricius respond to the doctor's offer to poison Pyrrhus?

11. What was the outcome of the Battle of Asculum?

12. Explain what is meant by a Pyrrhic victory.

Using Latin	**Ā fortiōrī** From the Latin meaning "from stronger (cause)", this expression is used to mean "more compelling".

CHAPTER 7
Relative clauses; more about "and"

Relative clauses

A relative clause begins with a word such as "who" or "which" (a relative pronoun) and tells us more about the noun or pronoun to which it refers.

E.g. The girl, *who was walking to school,*...
E.g. The hay-stack, *which we saw in the fields,*...

In these examples the words in italics are relative clauses, telling us more about the nouns (the girl and the hay-stack) to which they refer.

The relative pronoun in Latin is quī, quae, quod:

quī, quae, quod = who, which:		
	M	**F**	**N**
Nom.	quī	quae	quod
Acc.	quem	quam	quod
Gen.	cuius	cuius	cuius
Dat.	cui [1]	cui [1]	cui [1]
Abl.	quō	quā	quō
Nom.	quī	quae	quae
Acc.	quōs	quās	quae
Gen.	quōrum	quārum	quōrum
Dat.	quibus [2]	quibus [2]	quibus [2]
Abl.	quibus [2]	quibus [2]	quibus [2]

1. Diphthong (see Appendix, p.100, note 8) 2. or quīs

Antecedents

The noun to which a relative clause refers is called the **antecedent**. In Latin, the relative pronoun must agree with the antecedent in *gender* and *number*. Its *case* is determined by its grammatical relationship within the relative clause and will often be different to the case of the antecedent:

Antecedent   **Relative clause**

The woman (nom.), who (nom.) is walking...   fēmina quae ambulat

The woman (nom.), whom (acc.) we hear...   fēmina quam audīmus

The woman (nom.), whose (gen.) daughter we like...   fēmina cuius fīliam amāmus

The woman (nom.), to whom (dat.) we gave a present... fēmina cui dōnum dedimus

The woman (nom.), by whom (abl.) he was killed...   fēmina ā quā interfectus est

So you really want to learn Latin...

Exercise 7. 1
Read the information on the opposite page about relative clauses. Then translate into Latin:

1. The boy (nom.), who is singing...
2. The girl (nom.), who is walking...
3. Of the war, which we are waging...
4. With the boy, whom we see...
5. The women (nom.), to whom we give...
6. The farmers (nom.), who are working...
7. With the soldier, whose...
8. Of the consuls, by whom...

Exercise 7. 2
Identify, with brackets and squiggles, the antecedent, relative pronoun and relative clause in the following sentences, as shown in sentence 1. Then translate:

1. dominus, [qui est in hortō,] īrātus est.
2. puella, quae est in agrō, cantat.
3. bellum, quod* erat longum, fēminās terrēbat.
4. dominus, quem amāmus, miser est.
5. puella, quam in agrō vidēmus, cantat.
6. bellum, quod Rōmānī gerēbant, incolās terrēbat.
7. dominus, cuius servus fessus est, īrātus semper est.
8. puella, cuius māter dormit, semper cantat.
9. exercitus, cuius ducem omnēs timent, ad oppidum iter faciēbat.
10. iam dominus, cui dōnum dedistī, laetus est.

* One can confuse quod = "because" with quod = "which". Here it could be either!

Exercise 7. 3
Identify the antecedent, relative pronoun and relative clause in the following sentences. Then translate:

1. The master, [who was writing a book,] was happy.
2. The girl, who was preparing the table, was very angry.
3. The soldier, whom we saw, was fighting.
4. The woman, whom we had warned, departed.
5. The general, whose army was fighting, was very bold.
6. The goddess, to whom we were singing, was Minerva.
7. The inhabitants, by whom we were being watched, lived in the mountains.
8. The horses, which were in the field, were drinking water.
9. The rivers, which we saw, were very deep.
10. The foot-soldiers, whom the leader had led into the wood, were very tired.

Using Latin

Ad lib.
Ad lib. is short for ad libitum = "at pleasure",
i.e. without planning.

Translating relative clauses

Sentences which contain relative clauses can cause problems if you are not careful. The key to success lies in knowing when to translate the relative clause. It is really very simple. You almost always translate the relative clause immediately **after you have translated the antecedent**. If the antecedent is not in the nominative case, this will involve waiting until you have got to it. Just be patient!

E.g. dominum, **quī est in hortō**, vidēmus =
We see the master, **who is in the garden**.

E.g. māter puerī, **quī est in hortō**, cantābat =
The mother of the boy, **who is in the garden**, was singing.

E.g. epistolam amīcō meō, **quī est in Graeciā**, mīsī =
I have sent a letter to my friend, **who is in Greece**.

Vocabulary 7

Nouns

aurum, aurī, n.	gold	
manus, manūs, f.	hand (*or* band of men)	
mōs, mōris, m.	custom	
poēta, -ae, m.	poet	
prīnceps, prīncipis, c.	chief	
soror, sorōris, f.	sister	
templum, templī, n.	temple	
verbum, verbī, n.	word	

Prepositions

prō + abl.	on behalf of
super + acc.	over
trāns + acc.	across

Conjunctions

ac, atque	and

Verbs

incipiō, incipere, incēpī, inceptum	I begin
intellegō, -ere, intellēxī, intellēctum	I understand
moveō, movēre, mōvī, mōtum	I move, set in motion
stō, stāre, stetī, stătum	I stand

Adverbs

magnopere	greatly
mox	soon
quandŏ?	when?
sīc	thus

More words for 'and'

So far you have always used et or –que for "and", but there are a couple of other words: ac and atque. When joining words or clauses, ac or atque may be used, ac never being used before a vowel or h.

dux equitēs **ac** peditēs ad castra dūxit =
The general led his cavalry **and** infantry towards the camp.

agricola domum revēnit **atque** agrōs parāvit =
The farmer came back home **and** prepared his fields.

So you really want to learn Latin...

Exercise 7.4
Study the information on the left-hand page about translating relative clauses. Then translate into English:

1. Pyrrhus, quem incolae Ītaliae vocābant, rēx ɛpīrī erat.
2. Rōmānī cum incolīs, quōs rēx adiuvābat, pugnāverant.
3. crās librōs, quōs mihǐ dedistī, legam.
4. dux, cuius exercitum spectābāmus, rēx Pyrrhus est.
5. bellum contrā Gallōs, quī urbem oppugnāverant, gessimus.
6. manum per viās urbis, quam oppugnāverat, dūcēbās.
7. propter perīculum, quod omnēs magnopere timent, ā patriā fugimus.
8. aurum īn silvā, quae prope urbem est, invēnit.
9. soror ducis domum revēnit et mātrem monuit.
10. mōrēs patrum nostrōrum cīvēs optimōs, quī urbem amant, semper regent.

Exercise 7.5
Translate into Latin:

1. We love the woman who gave presents to us yesterday.
2. They watch the army which Pyrrhus is leading into the country.
3. The general has led a band of men into very great danger on behalf of his country.
4. He was reading the book which you gave to me.
5. We will stand near the gate which the citizens have built.
6. The chief, whom we had led to Rome, was killed by the guards during the night.
7. At first we will obey the new master who has completed the work.
8. After the citizens had departed, the Gauls entered the city.
9. The old men, who were not terrified by the enemy, remained in the forum.
10. The foot-soldiers will reply to the general within five days.

Exercise 7.6
Read the information on the left-hand page about 'and'. Then translate into English:

dum Rōmānī cum Pyrrhō bellum gerunt, cīvis Graecus captus est. is autem ad imperātōrem Rōmānum, nōmine Fabricium, vēnit ac sīc dīxit. "sī" inquit "multam pecūniam mihǐ dederis, rēgem Graecum interficiam."

verba tamen cīvis eius Fabricium nōn mōvērunt. "armīs," inquit "nōn perfidiā, Rōmānī hostēs superābunt." tum custōdī quī prope eum stābat "discēde" inquit "atque omnia rēgī nārrā!" rēx autem, quī magnopere mōtus est, multōs captīvōs Rōmānīs dedit.

perfidia, -ae, f. = treachery

** Using Latin** | **Prō ratā**
Prō ratā is short for prō ratā parte = according to the proportionate part, i.e. proportionately.

Enter the Carthaginians

Pyrrhus had been very impressed with the Romans and was not sorry when the opportunity was presented for bidding them farewell. The people of Sicily were having trouble with Carthage and wished someone to come and help them boot the Carthaginians out of their island. Pyrrhus gladly accepted the challenge and crossed over to Sicily.

Carthage, the town in north Africa where Aeneas had met Dido all those years before, was at this time the major sea power in the Mediterranean. Pyrrhus thought it would be a good idea to help the Sicilians, not because he wanted to help the Sicilians but because he thought that, if anyone was going to grab Sicily, he should be the one doing the grabbing, rather than the Carthaginians. However,

after three years or so he had had very little success in his attempt to dislodge the Carthaginians and so he returned to Italy. Here he resolved to march against the Romans once more, elephants and all. However, the Romans saw him coming and, at the Battle of Beneventum (275 B.C.), fired burning arrows and lighted barrels of tar in amongst the elephants. This caused chaos as the elephants stampeded back into their own troops and Pyrrhus, once more, learnt that fighting the Romans was not all it had been cracked up to be. He returned to Greece where he soon afterwards died, apparently hit on the head by a roof-tile thrown from a house-top by an angry woman in the city of Argos!

So you really want to learn Latin...

Exercise 7. 7
Read the information on the left-hand page and then answer the following questions in complete sentences:

1. Why did Pyrrhus leave Italy?
2. What were Pyrrhus's real motives for going to help the Sicilians against the Carthaginians?
3. What happened at the Battle of Beneventum (275 B.C.)?
4. What did Pyrrhus do after the battle?
5. How did Pyrrhus eventually die?

Exercise 7. 8
Revision. Translate:

1. He has been wounded
2. She has been warned
3. It has been carried
4. They have been killed
5. She will have been ordered

Exercise 7. 9
Revision. Translate:

1. cum mīlitibus audāciōribus
2. sub mēnsā maximā
3. īn silvam minimam
4. ab amīcō fēlīcissimō
5. opus difficile

Revision
Write down and learn by heart:

• Quī, quae, quod.
• The words in Vocabulary 7.
• Check that you have not forgotten is, ea, id!

Using Latin

Status quō
The status quō is the situation as it was (or is).

CHAPTER 8
Hic and ille; formation and comparison of adverbs

Hic and ille

You have already met the demonstrative pronoun is, ea, id = that. Now you're going to meet two other demonstrative pronouns, hic = this (near me) and ille = that (over there).

hic, haec, hoc = this (near me) [plural = these]		
M	**F**	**N**
Nom. hic	haec	hoc
Acc. hunc	hanc	hoc
Gen. huius	huius	huius
Dat. huic*	huic*	huic*
Abl. hōc	hāc	hōc
Nom. hī	hae	haec
Acc. hōs	hās	haec
Gen. hōrum	hārum	hōrum
Dat. hīs	hīs	hīs
Abl. hīs	hīs	hīs

* Diphthong, see Appendix on page 100, note 8.

ille, illa, illud = that (over there) [plural = those]		
M	**F**	**N**
Nom. ille	illa	illud
Acc. illum	illam	illud
Gen. illĭus	illĭus	illĭus
Dat. illī	illī	illī
Abl. illō	illā	illō
Nom. illī	illae	illa
Acc. illōs	illās	illa
Gen. illōrum	illārum	illōrum
Dat. illīs	illīs	illīs
Abl. illīs	illīs	illīs

Using hic and ille

1. Hic and ille work just like is, ea, id in that, when not used in agreement with a noun, they mean "he", "she" or "it".
   E.g. mīles hunc interfēcit = the soldier killed him (i.e. *this man here*).

2. Ille and hic may be used like "the former...the latter." In such cases, ille means the former (because further away in the sentence!) and hic means the latter (because nearer).
   E.g. Mārcus agricolam vīdit. ille erat īrātus, hic dormiēbat =
   Marcus saw the farmer. The *former* (i.e. Marcus) was angry, the *latter* (i.e. the farmer) was asleep.

So you really want to learn Latin...

Exercise 8. 1

Study the information on the opposite page about hic and ille. Then translate into Latin:

1. This soldier (nom.)

2. Those girls (acc.)

3. Of this war

4. For those boys

5. Of these masters

Exercise 8. 2

Translate into English:

1. illōrum agricolārum

2. haec bella

3. huius fēminae

4. ab illō magistrō

5. illārum cōpiārum

Exercise 8. 3

Study the information on the left-hand page about using hic and ille. Translate into Latin:

1. Those soldiers were attacking that city.

2. We understand these laws now.

3. Marcus and Brutus are soldiers. The former is brave but the latter is very proud.

4. Those kings have ruled this city for many years.

5. All the citizens were seeking peace on account of that danger.

6. He will leave those gifts on this table.

7. We will obey them.

8. That poet did not like him.

9. Why did you not depart from that country?

10. He was carrying the weapons through the streets of that city.

Exercise 8. 4

Translate into English:

Rōmānī tandem illōs hostēs ab Ītaliā fugere coēgērunt. rēx autem hostium, quī incolās adiuvāre cupīverat, exercitum in nāvēs dūxit domumque iter fēcit. Rōmānī iam omnem terram superāverant atque ab incolīs timēbantur. sed fāmam maiōrem semper cupiēbant et aliās terrās mox superāre cupiēbant. mīlitēs Rōmānī fortissimī erant et prō patriā saepe in nāvibus missī sunt.

Using Latin	**Ad hoc**
	Ad hoc = for this (purpose). E.g. an ad hoc committee is one set up to cope with a particular issue.

Formation of adverbs

Adverbs normally end in -ly in English and are used to describe verbs (e.g. "she sang beautifully"), adjectives (e.g. "amazingly clever") and even other adverbs (e.g. "amazingly well"). In Latin, they may be formed from adjectives as follows:

1st/2nd declension adjectives: add -ē or occasionally -ō to the stem.

E.g.
dignus = worthy	dignē = worthily
pulcher = beautiful	pulchrē = beautifully
tūtus = safe	tūtō = safely

3rd declension adjectives: add -iter, -ter or -er to the stem:

fortis = brave	fortiter = bravely
audāx = bold	audācter = boldly
cōnstāns = steady	cōnstanter = steadily

Some adjectives simply use their neuter singular:

multus = much	multum = much, a lot
facilis = easy	facile = easily

This may all look rather unhelpful, but it isn't too difficult, really.

1. The regular formation of adverbs from 1st/2nd declension adjectives is to add –ē to the stem. Those that add –ō are irregular and are not wildly common.

2. 3rd declension adjectives regularly add –iter to the stem, unless the stem ends in –nt, in which case they add –er. It is pure laziness on the part of audax to go audacter, and indeed the Romans themselves didn't seem too sure whether they should be saying audacter, as audaciter is also occasionally found (although it is rare).

3. The fact that some adjectives use their neuter singular is, indeed, a blow to morale. There's nothing you can do about this one, apart from learn those adjectives that do it.

Comparison of adverbs

1. The comparative of an adverb (e.g. "more bravely") is the same as the neuter singular of the comparative adjective.

2. The superlative of an adverb (e.g. "very bravely" or "most bravely") is the same as the superlative adjective but changing -us to -ē.

Thus, using the adjective rēctus = "right" and fortis = "brave", we can show the relationship between the adjective and the adverb as follows:

	Positive	Comparative	Superlative
Adjective:	rēctus, -a, um	rēctior, rēctius	rēctissimus, -a, -um
Adverb:	rēctē	rēctius	rēctissimē
Adjective:	fortis, forte	fortior, fortius	fortissimus, -a, -um
Adverb:	fortiter	fortius	fortissimē

So you really want to learn Latin...

Exercise 8. 5
Study the information on the opposite page about the formation and comparison of adverbs. Then translate into Latin:

1. Faithful, more faithful, most faithful
2. Faithfully, more faithfully, most faithfully
3. Fortunate, more fortunate, very fortunate
4. Fortunately, more fortunately, very fortunately
5. Beautiful, more beautiful, very beautiful
6. Beautifully, more beautifully, most beautifully

Exercise 8. 6
Translate into Latin:

1. The Romans have fought more bravely than the Gauls.
2. Those ships were destroyed by a very big storm.
3. At that time kings ruled wisely in the city.
4. We threw the spears more boldly.
5. He has handed over very many prisoners to the Roman general.
6. We have praised the courage of those brave men.
7. The enemy wanted to hand over many men to our leader.
8. Our men were conquered by the Gauls who fought very bravely.
9. The young man boldly placed his hand into the fire.
10. The citizens wanted to hand over gold and silver to the enemy very quickly.

Exercise 8. 7
Translate into English:

Rōmānī cum Graecīs fortiter pugnāvērunt neque tamen eōs vīcērunt. nam rēx Graecus, nōmine Pyrrhus, dux fortissimus erat et exercitum audācissimē in proelium dūcēbat. ōlim pedes Graecus captus et ad ducem Rōmānum missus est. hic pedes Rōmānīs "sī mihĭ" inquit "argentum aurumque dederitis, rēgem Graecum interficiam". Rōmānī tamen nōn mōtī sunt. "nōs Rōmānī" inquit dux Rōmānus "virtūte mīlitum et ingeniō ducis hostēs vincēmus. tuō rēgī mox tē trādam. fortasse ā mīlitibus tuīs interficiēris." ubĭ Pyrrhus verba Rōmānōrum audīvit magnopere mōtus est. "hōc modō," inquit "Rōmānī vincent et ego superābor."

	Rē
Using Latin	Rē is short for in rē = "in the matter (of)". E.g. "I am writing rē the advertisement in yesterday's paper".

Vocabulary 8

Nouns		Verbs	
argentum, argentī, n.	silver	incendō, -ere,	I set alight
incendium, incendiī, n.	a fire, blaze	incendī, incēnsum	
ingenium, ingeniī, n.	ability, talent	prōmittō, -ere,	I promise
modus, modī, m.	way, manner, means	prōmīsī, prōmissum	
		trādō, -ere,	I hand over
oculus, oculī, m.	eye	trādidī, trāditum	
tempestās, tempestātis, f.	storm, weather	trahō, trahere, traxī, tractum	I drag
tempus, tempŏris, n.	time	vertō, -ere,	I turn
uxor, uxōris, f.	wife	vertī, versum	
virtūs, virtūtis, f.	courage	vincō, -ere,	I conquer
vīta, vītae, f.	life	vīcī, victum	
Adverbs		**Adjective**	
quoque*	also, too	rēctus, -a, -um	right (i.e. not "wrong")
subitō	suddenly		

* quoque comes after the emphasised word. E.g. tū quoque = you too.

Irregular adverbs

The following irregular adverbs should be noted:

	Adverb	Comparative	Superlative
Well	benĕ	melius	optimē
Badly	malĕ	peius	pessimē
Greatly	magnopere	magis	maximē
Little	paulum	minus	minimē
Much	multum	plūs	plūrimum
Note also:			
For a long time	diū	diūtius	diūtissimē
After	post	posterius	postrēmō
Near, nearly	prope	propius	proximē
Often	saepe	saepius	saepissimē

Perfect and aorist

I've been meaning to tell you for a couple of chapters now, but, as in the active, the perfect passive tense has to double up as an aorist or "simple past". Thus, as well as meaning "I have been loved", amātus sum also means "I *was* loved".

E.g. mīles sagittā vulnerātus est = the soldier was wounded by the arrow.

You had probably worked this out for yourself, but there it is anyway.

So you really want to learn Latin...

Exercise 8. 8
Study the words in Vocabulary 8. From which Latin words are the following derived?
Explain the meaning of the English words and translate the Latin ones.

1. Victorious
2. Reverse
3. Tempestuous
4. Promise
5. Vitality
6. Trade
7. Traction
8. Incendiary
9. Mode
10. Oculist

Exercise 8. 9
Study the information on the left-hand page about irregular adverbs. Then translate into English:

1. cōnsul rēs urbis pessimē gessit.
2. mīlitēs Rōmānī in proeliō optimē pugnābant.
3. rēx Graecus verbīs ducis magnopere mōtus est.
4. māter fīliās saepissimē monēbat.
5. postrēmō dux castra prope flūmen posuit.

Exercise 8. 10
Revision. Translate the following into English.

1. audiet
2. regit
3. monēbāmur
4. audītus sum
5. caperis
6. capiēris
7. audīte
8. dūxī
9. dūcī
10. regere
11. esse
12. fuit
13. erant
14. sumus
15. pugnātis
16. in pugnā
17. in mare
18. in marī
19. sub cubīlī
20. post haec

Using Latin

Alumnus
An alumnus of a school or university is an ex-pupil.
In Latin, alumnus = "nursling" or "foster-child".

The story so far...

Time to recap, methinks, on the glorious story of Rome so far. Rome, as you have seen, was not built in a day but as we approach the next phase in her rise to world supremacy, and before we wheel on the Carthaginians, we can look back at some of the highlights in her rise from shepherd sanctuary to Italian superpower.

First (in Book I) we had Aeneas, escaping from the burning ashes of Troy, braving the perils of the seas, jilting the lovely Dido and overcoming the less lovely Turnus. His son, Ascanius, left home to build his own city and there, several generations later, the lovely Rhea Silvia had her little fling with the god Mars and out popped Romulus and Remus. Romulus disposed of his brother, founded Rome and then set about populating the new city with maidens seized from the Sabines. He then whizzed up to heaven and was succeeded by a succession of kings with odd sounding names, ending up with the dreaded Tarquin the Proud who was too proud and got evicted.

Then it was Horatius, bashing up the Etruscans as he fought valiantly to hold the bridge over the River Tiber. Mucius Scaevola then performed his flame-throwing trick and, as we moved into Book II, Cloelia went for a swim and Coriolanus had trouble with his mother.

The plebeians and the patricians then began squabbling and fathers took to murdering their daughters. The Gauls arrived and sacked the city but were chased away by some sacred geese. Manlius Torquatus got his silly name by wearing a Gallic necklace and fathers then turned from killing their daughters to killing their sons.

Next, Rome turned on the local Italians and then had to cope with the elephants of Pyrrhus before she was able at last to take a breather and say vēnimus, vīdimus, vīcimus, or words to that effect. Not bad for a little Italian town, I think you will agree. But what would happen when she decided that Italy was too small and that she wanted to rule the whole world? Stay tuned for the next exciting instalment...

So you really want to learn Latin...

Exercise 8. 11

Read the story on the opposite page, reminding you of what you have learnt so far about the history of Rome. Then answer the following questions in complete sentences, referring back to earlier chapters where necessary:

1. When was the Trojan War (approximately)?

2. When was Rome founded?

3. How did Romulus attract women into his city?

4. Who was the traitress who tried to let the Sabines into the city?

5. What was the name given to Romulus when he became a god?

6. How many kings of Rome were there between 753 and 510 B.C.?

7. After the expulsion of Tarquin the Proud, how was Rome ruled?

8. Which three Romans defended the bridge against the Etruscan army?

9. Who was the king in charge of the Etruscans at that time?

10. Why was Mucius Scaevola called *Scaevola*?

11. What happened to Cloelia when she swam safely back to Rome?

12. Why was Coriolanus's mother so angry with him?

13. Who were the patricians and the plebeians?

14. When was the Battle of Allia and who won?

15. When did the Gauls enter the city of Rome and kill the old senators?

16. Which Roman general saved Rome from the Gauls?

17. Which Roman general, much later, was responsible for the conquest of Gaul?

18. Why did Manlius Torquatus kill his son?

19. Who was Pyrrhus and what is meant by a pyrrhic victory?

20. Give *three* reasons why Fabricius was such a jolly good Roman.

| *Using Latin* | **Cōnsēnsus**
A cōnsēnsus is a "common feeling" or "agreement". |

CHAPTER 9
Deponent verbs; semi-deponent verbs

Deponent verbs of the 1st conjugation

Now for a particularly odd beast, the deponent verb. A deponent verb is *passive in form* but *active in meaning*. That is, it looks passive but should be translated as if it were active. E.g. cōnātur = he is trying; cōnātus sum = I have tried.

A deponent verb has only three principal parts. These can be compared to the passive of the regular verb as follows:

cōnor	cōnārī	cōnātus sum
I try	to try	I have tried
amor	amārī	amātus sum
I am loved	to be loved	I have been loved

You can tell to which conjugation a deponent verb belongs by studying its principal parts and comparing these to the passive of the regular conjugations. 1st conjugation deponent verbs have principal parts in -or, -ārī, -ātus sum:

cōnor, cōnārī, cōnātus sum = I try

Present		**Perfect**	
cōn-or	I try	cōnāt-us sum	I have tried
cōnā-ris	You (sing.) try	cōnāt-us es	You have tried
cōnā-tur	He, she, it tries	cōnāt-us est	He, she, it has tried
cōnā-mur	We try	cōnāt-ī sumus	We have tried
cōnā-minī	You (pl.) try	cōnāt-ī estis	You have tried
cōna-ntur	They try	cōnāt-ī sunt	They have tried
Future		**Future perfect**	
cōnā-bor	I shall/will try	cōnāt-us erō	I shall/will have tried
cōnā-beris	You (sing.) will try	cōnāt-us eris	You will have tried
cōnā-bitur	He, she, it will try	cōnāt-us erit	He, she, it will have tried
cōnā-bimur	We shall/will try	cōnāt-ī erimus	We shall/will have tried
cōnā-biminī	You (pl.) will try	cōnāt-ī eritis	You will have tried
cōnā-buntur	They will try	cōnāt-ī erunt	They will have tried
Imperfect		**Pluperfect**	
cōnā-bar	I was trying	cōnāt-us eram	I had tried
cōnā-bāris	You (sing.) were trying	cōnāt-us erās	You had tried
cōnā-bātur	He, she, it was trying	cōnāt-us erat	He, she, it had tried
cōnā-bāmur	We were trying	cōnāt-ī erāmus	We had tried
cōnā-bāminī	You (pl.) were trying	cōnāt-ī erātis	You had tried
cōnā-bantur	They were trying	cōnāt-ī erant	They had tried

As you would expect, the –us in the perfect stem tenses has to agree with the subject: E.g. the girl has tried = puella cōnāta est.

So you really want to learn Latin...

Exercise 9. 1

Study the information on the left-hand page about deponent verbs. Note that you must be familiar with the *passive infinitives* of regular verbs if you are to be able to recognise the conjugation of a deponent verb. Note that the tenses of a deponent verb are identical to the *passive* tenses of verbs of that conjugation. Now write out the following tenses:

1. amō in the present *passive*

2. mīror, mīrārī, mīrātus sum = "I wonder at" in the present tense

3. amō in the future *passive*

4. hortor, hortārī, hortātus sum = "I encourage" in the future tense

5. amō in the imperfect *passive*

6. moror, morārī, morātus sum = "I delay" in the imperfect tense

Exercise 9. 2

Write out the following tenses:

1. Perfect *passive* of amō

2. Perfect tense of hortor

3. Future perfect *passive* of amō

4. Future perfect tense of mīror

5. Pluperfect *passive* of amō

6. Pluperfect tense of moror

Exercise 9. 3

Translate into Latin:

1. He is encouraging the farmers.

2. We were wondering at the boy.

3. They were trying to find the camp.

4. I will encourage my soldiers.

5. She wondered at the many gifts.

6. You (sing.) were trying to encourage me for many hours.

7. On the fifth day he will encourage his daughter.

8. The angry women have encouraged the boy.

9. The soldiers tried to fight more bravely than the enemy.

10. The general has delayed because of the storm.

Using Latin	**In perpetuum** In perpetuum = "for ever". The Latin adjective perpetuus = "continuing throughout".

Deponent verbs of the 2nd conjugation

Second conjugation verbs have principal parts in –eor, –ērī and go like the passive of moneō.

vereor, verērī, veritus sum = I fear

Present		Perfect	
vere-or	I fear	verit-us sum	I have feared
verē-ris	You (sing.) fear	verit-us es	You (sing.) have feared
verē-tur	He, she, it fears	verit-us est	He, she, it has feared
verē-mur	We fear	verit-ī sumus	We have feared
verē-minī	You (pl.) fear	verit-ī estis	You (pl.) have feared
vere-ntur	They fear	verit-ī sunt	They have feared
Future		**Future perfect**	
verē-bor	I shall/will fear	verit-us erō	I shall/will have feared
verē-beris	You (sing.) will fear	verit-us eris	You (sing.) will have feared
verē-bitur	He, she, it will fear	verit-us erit	He will have feared
verē-bimur	We shall/will fear	verit-ī erimus	We shall/will have feared
verē-biminī	You (pl.) will fear	verit-ī eritis	You (pl.) will have feared
verē-buntur	They will fear	verit-ī erunt	They will have feared
Imperfect		**Pluperfect**	
verē-bar	I was fearing	verit-us eram	I had feared
verē-bāris	You (sing.) were fearing	verit-us erās	You (sing.) had feared
verē-bātur	He, she, it was fearing	verit-us erat	He, she, it had feared
verē-bāmur	We were fearing	verit-ī erāmus	We had feared
verē-bāminī	You were fearing	verit-ī erātis	You (pl.) had feared
verē-bantur	They were fearing	verit-ī erant	They had feared

Semi-deponent verbs

If you thought deponent verbs were odd, take a look at semi-deponent ones. Semi-deponent verbs are active in form in those tenses which are formed on the *present stem*, but passive in form when they get into the *perfect stem* tenses:

E.g. gaudeō, gaudēre, gāvīsus sum = I rejoice
    audeō, audēre, ausus sum = I dare
    soleō, solēre, solitus sum = I am accustomed

The six tenses of gaudeō thus begin:

Present	gaudeō	Perfect	gāvīsus sum
Future	gaudēbō	Future perfect	gāvīsus erō
Imperfect	gaudēbam	Pluperfect	gāvīsus eram

So you really want to learn Latin...

Exercise 9. 4

Read the information on the left-hand page about deponent verbs of the 2nd conjugation. Note that the verb videor is both the passive of videō, and can thus be translated as "I am seen"; and also a deponent verb in its own right meaning "I seem". Now give the Latin for:

1. He seems to be happy.
2. She has been seen in the garden.
3. They seem to like the story.
4. They will be seen by the farmer's wife.
5. She does not like to be seen.

Exercise 9. 5

Read the information on the left-hand page about semi-deponent verbs. Be sure always to translate semi-deponent verbs with an *active* meaning, even though they look passive in the perfect stem tenses. Now translate into English:

1. Rōmānī urbem oppugnāre nōn audēbunt.
2. Gallī īn silvīs pugnāre solēbant.
3. puellae Rōmānae mātrēs adiuvāre solitae erant.
4. omnēs propter victōriam gaudēbant.
5. poēta propter carmina sua laudātus est.
6. postquam nūntiī discessērunt omnēs incolae gāvīsī sunt.

Exercise 9. 6

Revision of verbs. Translate into English:

1. monent
2. monentur
3. regent
4. regentur
5. audiēmus
6. audiēmur
7. cēpit
8. capit
9. capiet
10. vident

11. vidēminī
12. vīsum est
13. vīsa est
14. amārī
15. incēpī
16. incipī
17. capī
18. fuī
19 esse
20. interficeris

	Parī passū
Using Latin	Parī passū = "with equal pace", i.e. simultaneously and equally.

Deponent verbs of the 3rd, 4th and mixed conjugations

You have now seen how deponent verbs take their endings from the *passive* of the regular conjugations. As we have said, if you know your passive infinitives, you should have no trouble identifying the conjugation of a deponent verb and if you know your passive endings you should know how it goes. Examples of 3rd, 4th and mixed conjugation deponent verbs are shown below:

3rd: loquor, loquī, locūtus sum = I speak
4th: partior, partīrī, partītus sum = I share
Mixed: morior, morī, mortuus sum = I die

Present

loqu-or = I speak	parti-or = I share	mori-or = I die
loqu-eris	partī-ris	mor-eris
loqu-itur	partī-tur	mor-itur
loqu-imur	partī-mur	mor-imur
loqu-iminī	partī-minī	mor-iminī
loqu-untur	parti-untur	mori-untur

Future

loqu-ar	parti-ar	mori-ar
loqu-ēris	parti-ēris	mori-ēris
loqu-ētur	parti-ētur	mori-ētur
loqu-ēmur	parti-ēmur	mori-ēmur
loqu-ēminī	parti-ēminī	mori-ēminī
loqu-entur	parti-entur	mori-entur

Imperfect

loqu-ēbar	parti-ēbar	mori-ēbar
loqu-ēbāris	parti-ēbāris	mori-ēbāris
loqu-ēbātur	parti-ēbātur	mori-ēbātur
loqu-ēbāmur	parti-ēbāmur	mori-ēbāmur
loqu-ēbāminī	parti-ēbāminī	mori-ēbāminī
loqu-ēbantur	parti-ēbantur	mori-ēbantur

Intransitive verbs in the passive

As you know, intransitive verbs are verbs which cannot govern a direct object (e.g. I walk, I swim, etc.) Note that some verbs which are transitive in English are intransitive in Latin, e.g. pugnō = "I fight" (in Latin, one never "fights someone", one "fights *with* someone"). An intransitive verb can only be used in the passive *impersonally* (i.e. the subject of the verb is the word "it").

E.g. pugnātum est = it was fought, i.e. there was fighting.

N.B. this also applies to verbs which take the dative, e.g. persuādeō.
E.g. I persuade you = tibĭ persuādeō; but
    I am persuaded by you = mihĭ persuādētur ā tē (i.e. it is persuaded to me by you).

So you really want to learn Latin...

Exercise 9. 7

Read the information on the left-hand page about deponent verbs of the 3rd, 4th and mixed conjugations. Then translate into English:

1. Rōmānī ad castra hostium prōgrediēbantur.

2. omnēs verba mīlitis mīrantur.

3. dominus servīs miserīs īrāscēbātur.

4. nōnne hostēs multīs sagittīs ūtentur*?

5. lēgātī in forō loquī cupiēbant.

* N.B. ūtor + abl. = "I use". This verb governs the ablative case, i.e. its object goes in the ablative rather than the accusative case.

Exercise 9. 8

Translate into Latin:

1. In the war soldiers will die every day.

2. The enemy seemed to fight more bravely than the Romans.

3. A great storm arose on the third day.

4. We used* our swords but at last were captured by the guards.

5. You (pl.) will follow the leader of the army into the hills.

* See note above about ūtor + abl.

Exercise 9. 9

Study the information on the left-hand page about intransitive verbs in the passive. Then translate into English: *The story of Regulus, 249 B.C.*

Rōmānī cum Poenīs pugnābant. dux autem Rōmānōrum, nōmine Rēgulus, multās victōriās peperit sed Carthāginem nōn cēperat. Rēgulus igitur mīlitēs ita allocūtus est: "num Rōmānī" inquit "ab hostibus superābuntur? omnis Ītalia ā Rōmānīs nunc victa est. īnsula Sicilia ōlim ab hostibus regēbātur, nunc tamen ā nōbīs regitur. nōs ad arma, nōs ad fāmam maximam vocāmur. ubĭ sōl iterum ortus erit, in urbe hostium cēnābimus."

in campō multās hōrās pugnābātur sed Rōmānī ab hostibus tandem superātī sunt. multī prō patriā mortuī sunt, sed Rēgulus captus et in urbem est ductus. post hoc lēgātī Rōmam missī sunt, inter quōs erat Rēgulus. hic, antequam profectus est, prō pāce loquī iussus est. Rēgulō tamen nōn persuāsum est. in forum Rōmānum ingressus est et prō bellō locūtus est. "arma Pūnica nōn timeō" inquit "nec pācem habēre cum hostibus cupiō. nunc ad hostēs regrediar et prō patriā moriar." ita Rōmānus fortis amīcōs relīquit et ad barbarōs regressus est.

victōriam pariō, -ere, peperī, partum = I win a victory
alloquor, alloquī, allocūtus sum = I address.

Using Latin

Nōn sequitur
A nōn sequitur is a statement which *does not follow*, logically, that which has preceded it.

alius = other

The Latin for "other" is alius, alia, aliud, e.g. "with another friend" = cum aliō amīcō.

	M	F	N	M	F	N
Nom.	alius	alia	aliud	aliī	aliae	alia
Acc.	alium	aliam	aliud	aliōs	aliās	alia
Gen.	alī̆us*	alī̆us*	alī̆us*	aliōrum	aliārum	aliōrum
Dat.	aliī**	aliī**	aliī**	aliīs	aliīs	aliīs
Abl.	aliō	aliā	aliō	aliīs	aliīs	aliīs

*Alterī̆us, the gen. sing. of alter (see below), is normally used in place of alī̆us.
**Alterī, the dat. sing. of alter (see below), is normally used in place of aliī.

alter = other (of two)

If "other" refers to the "other *of two*" (e.g. the other leg), then alter is used rather than alius:

	M	F	N	M	F	N
Nom.	alter	altera	alterum	alterī	alterae	altera
Acc.	alterum	alteram	alterum	alterōs	alterās	altera
Gen.	alterī̆us	alterī̆us	alterī̆us	alterōrum	alterārum	alterōrum
Dat.	alterī	alterī	alterī	alterīs	alterīs	alterīs
Abl.	alterō	alterā	alterō	alterīs	alterīs	alterīs

cēterī = others (the rest)

If "others" means "the rest" or "remaining", we use cēterī, -ae, -a. E.g. Horatius was fighting but the others had fled = Horātius pugnābat sed cēterī fūgerant.

Vocabulary 9

Verbs

audeō, -ēre, ausus sum	I dare	prōgredior, prōgredī,	I advance,
cēnō, -āre, -āvī, -ātum	I dine	prōgressus sum	go forward
cōnor, -ārī, cōnātus sum	I try	sequor, sequī, secūtus sum	I follow
gaudeō, -ēre, gāvīsus sum	I rejoice	ūtor, ūtī, ūsus sum (+ abl.)	I use
īrāscor, īrāscī,	I am angry	videor, vidērī, vīsus sum	I seem
īrātus sum (+ dat.)	(with)	**Adjectives**	
loquor, loquī, locūtus sum	I speak	alius, alia, aliud	other
mīror, -ārī, mīrātus sum	I wonder at,	alter, altera, alterum	other (of two)
	am amazed	cēterī, -ae, -a	other, the rest,
morior, morī, mortuus sum	I die		remaining
nāscor, nāscī, nātus sum	I am born	**Preposition**	
orior*, orīrī, ortus sum	I arise	apud + acc.	at the house of
proficīscor, proficīscī,	I set out	**Adverb**	
profectus sum		cōtīdiē	every day

* Despite its present infinitive, orior is a mixed conjugation verb.

So you really want to learn Latin...

Exercise 9. 10
Study the information on the left-hand page about the three ways of translating "other".
Then translate into Latin:

1. After the battle the enemy general adopted another plan.
2. We set out before the others had won another victory.
3. After the Romans had adopted this plan, the other citizens rejoiced.
4. The bravest soldiers were fighting for many hours but the others had fled.
5. We used to dine at the house of the other consul every day.

Exercise 9. 11
Study the words in Vocabulary 9. Note that compounds of gradior (e.g. prōgredior, ingredior, ēgredior, etc.) are very common. From which Latin words do the following English ones derive? Translate the Latin word and explain the meaning of the English one:

1. Alternative
2. Sequence
3. Progress
4. Irascible
5. Loquacious
6. Mortuary
7. Orient
8. Admirable
9. Ingress
10. Egress

Exercise 9. 12
Verb revision. Translate into Latin:

1. We are loved
2. They have been loved
3. You (sing.) will be loved
4. She was being warned
5. You (pl.) will be warned
6. He had been warned
7. We will rule
8. I will be ruled
9. She will have ruled
10. They have been heard
11. To be heard
12. He is
13. It will be
14. They were
15. To be
16. We have been
17. He takes
18. They are being taken
19. To be captured
20. Be warned! (plural)

Alter egŏ
Alter egŏ = another self. An alter egŏ is a close friend or soul-mate.

Using Latin

The first Punic War 264-241 B.C.

We have now seen how Rome grew from a small town, harbouring a group of shepherds and runaway slaves, into a city controlling the whole of Italy. In 264 BC Rome launched its first war outside Italy, against the city of Carthage. Carthage was at that time the strongest power in the western Mediterranean with an empire comprising the coastlands of north Africa, southern Spain, Sardinia, Corsica and western Sicily. In 264, the people of Messana in Sicily appealed to the Romans for help in evicting a Carthaginian force, which had proved rather slow in leaving, after having come to help Messana in a war with her neighbour, Syracuse. The Romans sent an army which drove the Carthaginians out of Messana and then, buoyed up by this success, they decided to drive the Carthaginians out of Sicily altogether. At the battle of Mylae in 260 they destroyed the Carthaginian fleet and then, after some futile attacks on Carthaginian outposts in Corsica and Sardinia, they decided to strike at Carthage itself. In 255 the Roman general Regulus, after getting within a mile of the city of Carthage, was captured in battle and his army destroyed. However, the

Carthaginians were unable to capitalise on this success and, a few years later, they sued for peace, sending Regulus back to Rome to obtain favourable terms from Rome.

Regulus, however, was a well brought up Roman and refused to encourage the Roman senate to break off the war with Carthage. He thus spoke in favour of continuing the war and then returned to Carthage to face certain death at the hands of the Carthaginians.

After this, Carthage sent a general called Hamilcar to Sicily. After marching around Sicily for a while, Hamilcar secured the strongholds of Mount Hercte and Mount Eryx but was then handicapped by lack of reinforcements and was defeated by the Romans at a sea battle off Drepana. In 241, the Carthaginians again sued for peace, renounced all claims to Sicily and agreed to pay a huge indemnity of 3,200 talents. Here endeth the first Punic War.

So you really want to learn Latin...

Exercise 9. 13
Read the information about the first Punic War and then answer the following questions in complete sentences.

1. When and against whom was the first Punic War fought?
2. Why did the people of Messana appeal to the Romans for help in 264?
3. What did the Romans decide to do after pushing the Carthaginians out of Messana?
4. When was the Battle of Mylae and what was the result of the battle?
5. What happened to Regulus and his army in 255?
6. In what ways did Regulus show his courage after he had been sent back to Rome?
7. How might this story have been used to inspire later generations of Romans?
8. Who was Hamilcar and what successes did he enjoy in Sicily?
9. How did the war end and what were the terms of the peace?
10. Draw a map of the Mediterranean, showing the areas controlled by Rome and those controlled by Carthage in 264 B.C.

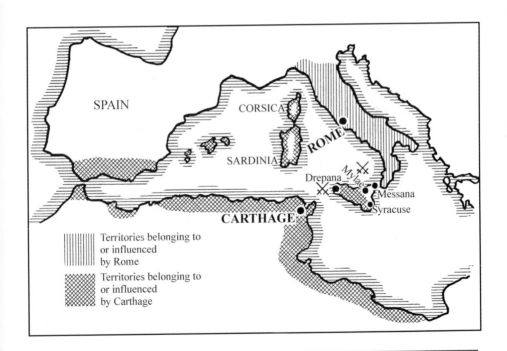

Using Latin	**Dulce et decōrum est prō patriā morī** Borrowed by Wilfred Owen from the Roman poet Horace: "It is sweet and beautiful to die for one's country".

Chapter 10
Irregular verbs; ipse *and* īdem

Irregular verbs: possum, ēo and ferō

A number of verbs in Latin are irregular. Three of the most common are:
possum, posse, potuī = I am able;
eō, īre, iī (or īvī), itum = I go; and, with the silliest principal parts in the language,
ferō, ferre, tŭlī, lātum = I carry, bear.

Present		[Active	Passive]
possum	eō	fero	feror
potes	īs	fers	ferris
potest	it	fert	fertur
possumus	īmus	ferimus	ferimur
potestis	ītis	fertis	feriminī
possunt	eunt	ferunt	feruntur
Future			
poterō	ībō	feram	ferar
poteris	ībis	ferēs	ferēris
poterit	ībit	feret	ferētur
poterimus	ībimus	ferēmus	ferēmur
poteritis	ībitis	ferētis	ferēminī
poterunt	ībunt	ferent	ferentur
Imperfect			
poteram	ībam	ferēbam	ferēbar
poterās	ībās	ferēbās	ferēbāris
poterat	ībat	ferēbat	ferēbātur
poterāmus	ībāmus	ferēbāmus	ferēbāmur
poterātis	ībātis	ferēbātis	ferēbāminī
poterant	ībant	ferēbant	ferēbantur

1. Possum is the result of a merger between the adjective potis = "able" and sum = "I am". It may be formed by putting pot- in front of the verb form, except where this begins with s, in which case it puts pos-.
2. Eō and ferō in the present just have to be learnt. After that, it's really just a matter of remembering whether they are bō, bis, bit verbs or am, ēs, et ones.

Compounds of eō

Compounds of eō are common: ineō = I go in; exeō = I go out; adeō = I approach; redeō = I go back, return; etc. With such compound verbs, the -iī form of the perfect tense is either the more common or, as with redeō, the *only* form.

So you really want to learn Latin...

Exercise 10. 1
Study the information on the left-hand page about irregular verbs. Then translate into Latin, using possum, eō or ferō:

1. He is able
2. They were carrying
3. They will be able
4. We are being carried
5. You (sing.) are carrying
6. It will be borne
7. We were going
8. We were not able
9. She will go
10. I will be able

Exercise 10. 2
Study the information on the left-hand page about compounds of eō. Then translate into English:

1. adeunt
2. inībant
3. potestis
4. ferre
5. poterāmus
6. exit
7. posse
8. feriminī
9. ferēminī
10. adīre

Exercise 10. 3
Translate into English:

1. crās aquam extrā mūrōs ferent.
2. herī cibum domum imperātōris ferēbātis.
3. mīlitēs Rōmānī capere Carthāginem nōn poterant.
4. Rēgulus dolōrem apud Poenōs ferre poterat.
5. nōnne īn silvam redībis et aquam ad urbem portābis?

Exercise 10. 4
Translate into Latin:

1. The young man was able to bear the pain for a long time.
2. First we will approach the house of the ambassador.
3. Were you carrying the arms to the Roman soldiers?
4. Money was being brought to the children of the king.
5. Are you able to overcome the enemy, soldiers?

Using Latin

Ipsō factō
Ipsō factō = by the fact itself. E.g.: "By murdering the man, she revealed, ipsō factō, her hatred for him".

Irregular verbs in the perfect

Conjugating an irregular verb in the perfect tense, or the future perfect or pluperfect for that matter, is no harder than it is with a regular verb. Just use the perfect stem and off you go!

E.g. for possum: potuī, potuistī, potuit, etc.

E.g. for ferō: tulī, tulistī, tulit, etc.

Eō in the perfect is normally iī, īstī, iit, etc. The forms īvī, īvistī, īvit etc. also occur, but are more rare.

Ipse and īdem

Ipse = "self" is something called an intensive pronoun, while īdem = "the same" is a definitive pronoun.

E.g. The women themselves = fēminae ipsae.

E.g. The same women = fēminae eaedem.

Ipse and īdem decline as follows:

	M	F	N	M	F	N
Nom.	ipse	ipsa	ipsum	īdem	eadem	idem
Acc.	ipsum	ipsam	ipsum	eundem	eandem	idem
Gen.	ipsĭus	ipsĭus	ipsĭus	eiusdem	eiusdem	eiusdem
Dat.	ipsī	ipsī	ipsī	eīdem	eīdem	eīdem
Abl.	ipsō	ipsā	ipsō	eōdem	eādem	eōdem
Nom.	ipsī	ipsae	ipsa	eīdem/īdem	eaedem	eadem
Acc.	ipsōs	ipsās	ipsa	eōsdem	eāsdem	eadem
Gen.	ipsōrum	ipsārum	ipsōrum	eōrundem	eārundem	eōrundem
Dat.	ipsīs	ipsīs	ipsīs	eīsdem*	eīsdem*	eīsdem*
Abl.	ipsīs	ipsīs	ipsīs	eīsdem*	eīsdem*	eīsdem*

*or īsdem.

More on imperatives

Just as a verb can have a passive infinitive ("to be loved", etc.), so it can have a passive imperative ("be loved!", "be warned!" etc.). Passive imperatives are formed as follows:
* Singular: identical to the present infinitive active:
  amāre, monēre, regere, audīre, capere.
* Plural: identical to the 2nd person plural, present passive:
  amāminī, monēminī, regiminī, audīminī, capiminī.

You should also know the following irregular imperatives (some of which you have already met):

es, este = be!	fac, facite = do!	fer, ferte = carry!
dūc, dūcite = lead!	ī, īte = go!	ferre, feriminī = be carried!
dīc, dīcite = say!		

So you really want to learn Latin...

Exercise 10. 5
Read the information on the left-hand page about irregular verbs in the perfect. Then translate into Latin, using ferō, not portō, where appropriate:

1. They have carried
2. You (sing.) have gone
3. She has been able
4. We have borne
5. You (pl.) will have gone out

6. They had carried
7. I will have been carried
8. He will have carried
9. You (sing.) have gone in
10. They have returned home

Exercise 10. 6
Study the information on the left-hand page about ipse and īdem and imperatives. Then translate:

1. custōdēs ipsōs custōdiet.
2. eīdem mīlitēs iterum pugnābunt.
3. rēx ipse in bellum festīnāvit.
4. pecūnia ā servīs eīsdem lāta est.
5. urbs ā rēge eōdem regēbātur.
6. Be brave, soldiers!
7. Marcus, lead the slaves home!
8. Carry the water into the town itself, boy! (Using ferō, not portō).
9. Flavia, lead the same girls out of the city!
10. Say those words to the king himself, Brutus!

Exercise 10. 7
Translate into English: *The end of the first Punic War, 242 B.C.*

postquam Rēgulus Carthāginem rediit, Poenī bellum cum Rōmānīs iterum gerēbant. imperātōrem, nōmine Hamilcarem, in Siciliam mīsērunt. ille autem illinc exercitum in Italiam dūxit. victōriās prope montēs <u>Herctem</u> et <u>Erycem</u> Hamilcar mox peperit. Rōmānī igitur cōpiās trāns īnsulam dūxērunt et hostēs aggressī sunt. Poenī paucissimōs mīlitēs habēbant sed diū Rōmānōrum <u>impetūs</u> <u>sustinēre</u> poterant. tandem tamen Rōmānī classem parāvērunt et Poenōs, quī multās nāvēs domum iam mīserant, prope <u>Drepana</u> superāvērunt. Poenī victī sunt et pācem petīvērunt. ē Siciliā discessērunt nec post hoc proelium regressī sunt.

Herctēs, Herctis, m. = Mt. Hercte; Eryx, Erycis, m. = Mt. Eryx; impetus, -ūs, m. = an attack; sustineō, -ēre = I withstand; Drepana, -ōrum, n. pl. = Drepana.

Using Latin

Quis custōdiet ipsōs custōdēs?
"Who will guard the guards themselves?" – a famous question put by the Roman poet Juvenal in the 1st c. A.D.

Vocabulary 10

Verbs

cūrō, -āre, -āvī, -ātum	I look after
eō, īre, iī (īvī), itum	I go
ferō, ferre, tŭlī, lātum	I carry, bear
possum, posse, potuī	I am able

Nouns

equĕs, equitis, m.	horseman
gaudium, -iī, n.	joy
īra, -ae, f.	anger
labor, labōris, m.	work
mors, mortis, f.	death
nēmŏ, nūllĭus, c. (irreg.)	no one

Pronouns

īdem, eadem, idem	the same
ipse, ipsa, ipsum	self

Adverbs

hīc	here
hinc	from here (hence)
hūc	to here (hither)
etiam	also, even
illīc	there
illinc	from there (thence)
intereā	meanwhile
illūc	to there (thither)
nōn sōlum...	not only...
sed etiam	but also

Preposition

extrā + acc.	outside

nēmŏ

nēmŏ = "no one" is an irregular noun declining as follows:
nēmŏ, nēmŏ, nēminem, nūllĭus, nēminī, nūllō.
The genitive and ablative forms are borrowed from the adjective nūllus = "no" (which declines like ūnus).

Can you do possum?

The English word "can" is translated into Latin using possum = "I am able", followed by an infinitive.
E.g. I can walk (I am able to walk) = ambulāre possum.
    Can you walk? (Are you able to walk?) = potesne ambulāre?

quam + superlative

The phrase "as...as possible" is translated into Latin by quam + a superlative.
E.g. quam celerrimē = as quickly as possible.
    quam fortissimē = as bravely as possible.

Here, there and everywhere

Notice how Latin likes to distinguish between "here", "to here" and "from here"; and between "there", "to there" and "from there". English used to do this (before we wrecked the language) by using the wonderful words "hither", "hence", "thither" and "thence". Thus hīc (rhyming with squeak) means "here" (in this place); but if you wish to say "come here!" you should say venī hūc (i.e. "come hither", or "to here"). Thus illīc (also rhyming with squeak) means "there" (in that place); but "hurry there!" = festīnā illūc! (i.e. "hurry thither", or "to there").

So you really want to learn Latin...

Exercise 10. 8
Study the information on the left-hand page. Then translate into Latin:

1. The king himself set out at dawn[1].

2. The same king looked after his horsemen for five days.

3. We will set out from here and go there.

4. Regulus himself did not fear the Carthaginians.

5. We cannot bear the anger of the gods.

6. No one can trust the son of the consul.

7. He can always give tasks to the same slaves.

8. The joy of the mother was greater than the pain of her son.

9. We shall set out as quickly as possible[2] towards the camp.

10. The cavalry can advance from there on to the plain.

N.B.   1. prīmā lūce = "at first light", i.e. "at dawn".
         2. See note on quam + superlative on left-hand page.

Exercise 10. 9
Using the words from Vocabulary 10 and elsewhere, say from which Latin words the following English ones derive. Translate the Latin word and explain the meaning of the English one:

1. Possible
2. Transfer
3. Mortality
4. Laborious
5. Cure

6. Exit
7. Extra
8. Ire
9. Curator
10. Refer

Exercise 10. 10
Translate into Latin:

For many years the forces of Rome waged war with the people of Italy. Once, a Greek king, called Pyrrhus, came to Italy with a large army. He brought help to the enemies of Rome, but in vain. After this the Romans feared the forces of Carthage and wanted to destroy them. Regulus led his soldiers into Africa but was captured. Then the war was waged in Sicily again. But at last the general of the Carthaginians, called Hamilcar, was forced to fight with the Romans by sea and was defeated.

Using Latin

| **In absentiā** |
| In absentiā = In (his/her) absence. For example: "We thanked the chairman in absentiā. |

The second Punic War, 218-201 B.C.

After their success in the first Punic War, Rome became distracted by a war with the hairy Gauls. Carthage took the opportunity to expand into Spain, seeking new sources of revenue to recoup her losses. Under the leadership, first of Hamilcar, then Hamilcar's son-in-law Hasdrubal, and finally Hamilcar's own son, Hannibal, the Carthaginians made inroads into Spain. This eventually came to the attention of the Romans in 219, when the town of Saguntum appealed to Rome for help against Hannibal's army. The following year, war was declared.

Rome went into the new war with a marked lack of urgency and was quite unprepared for the audacity of the young Hannibal. Hannibal had inherited his passionate hatred of the Romans from his father, Hamilcar, who had made him swear on oath that he would never make friends with the Romans. Hannibal never forgot this oath. Now, aged 25 and knowing that the obvious route into Italy was by sea from the south, Hannibal decided to try something different. He marched his army of around 50,000 men and a number of elephants through Spain, up over the Alps and down the other side into Italy.

Having reached Italy in this rather spectacular fashion, Hannibal beat the Romans at the Battles of Trebia and Lake Trasimene, leaving the route through to Rome clear. In Book III, if you can stand the suspense, we will see what happened next.

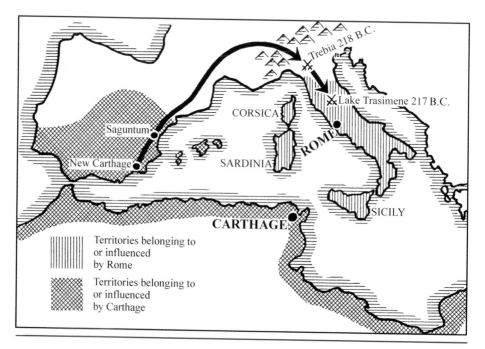

Territories belonging to or influenced by Rome

Territories belonging to or influenced by Carthage

So you really want to learn Latin...

Exercise 10. 11

Read the information on the left-hand page about the second Punic War and then answer the following questions in complete sentences:

1. Give the dates of the second Punic War.

2. Why was Carthage interested in expanding into Spain at this time?

3. Why was Rome slow to do anything about this?

4. How were the three Carthaginian generals responsible for the war in Spain related?

5. What happened in 219 B.C.?

6. How had Hamilcar demonstrated to his son the importance of the war against Rome?

7. In what way was the composition of Hannibal's army somewhat unusual?

8. Describe Hannibal's route into Italy.

Exercise 10. 12

Just to check that you have been putting your amazing knowledge of Latin to good use, what do the following mean?

1. vāde mēcum
2. compos mentis
3. cōgitō, ergŏ sum
4. vēnī, vīdī, vīcī
5. bona fidēs

6. carpe diem
7. alma māter
8. ā fortiōrī
9. prō ratā
10. ad hoc

Using Latin

Avē atque valē
A suitable one with which to finish,
avē atque valē = Hello and goodbye!

BEFORE WE MOVE ON... Latin checklist

Success in Latin can be put down to your skill (or lack of it) in three key areas: grammar, vocabulary and translating. If you don't know any vocabulary, you won't be able to translate anything. If you don't know any grammar, you won't be able to translate anything with any degree of accuracy. Finally, if you have forgotten your rules for translating, you will find it very hard to write anything which sounds like English or Latin. So, before we move on to Book III, go through the following list and tick off the things you are happy with.

Vocabulary

☐ Book I, Vocabulary 1
☐ Book I, Vocabulary 2
☐ Book I, Vocabulary 3
☐ Book I, Vocabulary 4
☐ Book I, Vocabulary 5
☐ Book I, Vocabulary 6
☐ Book I, Vocabulary 7
☐ Book I, Vocabulary 8
☐ Book I, Vocabulary 9
☐ Book I, Vocabulary 10

☐ Book II, Vocabulary 1
☐ Book II, Vocabulary 2
☐ Book II, Vocabulary 3
☐ Book II, Vocabulary 4
☐ Book II, Vocabulary 5
☐ Book II, Vocabulary 6
☐ Book II, Vocabulary 7
☐ Book II, Vocabulary 8
☐ Book II, Vocabulary 9
☐ Book II, Vocabulary 10

Grammar

1. Verbs

☐ Amō, six tenses active
☐ Moneō, six tenses active
☐ Regō, six tenses active
☐ Audiō, six tenses active
☐ Capiō, six tenses active
☐ Present infinitives, active
☐ Present imperatives, active

☐ Amō, six tenses passive
☐ Moneō, six tenses passive
☐ Regō, six tenses passive
☐ Audiō, six tenses passive
☐ Capiō, six tenses passive
☐ Present infinitives, passive
☐ Present imperatives, passive

2. Irregular verbs

☐ Sum, six tenses active
☐ Eō, six tenses active

☐ Possum, six tenses active
☐ Ferō, six tenses active and passive

3. Nouns

☐ 1st dec.: mēnsa
☐ 2nd dec. in –us: annus
☐ 2nd dec., neuter: bellum
☐ 2nd dec. in –er: puer and magister
☐ 2nd dec., irreg.: fīlius, deus and vir
☐ 3rd dec., increasing: rēx

☐ 3rd dec., neuter, increasing: opus
☐ 3rd dec., non-increasing: cīvis
☐ 3rd dec., neuter, non-increasing: cubīle
☐ 4th dec.: gradus
☐ 4th dec., neuter: genū
☐ 5th dec.: rēs and diēs

4. Adjectives and adverbs

☐ 1st/2nd declension in –us, -a, -um: bonus
☐ 1st/2nd declension in –er: tener and pulcher
☐ 3rd declension, one termination: ingēns
☐ 3rd declension, two termination: trīstis
☐ 3rd declension, three termination: ācer

- ☐ Comparative adjectives in –ior: melior
- ☐ Numerals: ūnus, duo, trēs
- ☐ Pronominal adjectives: alius and alter
- ☐ The comparison of adjectives, regular
- ☐ The comparison of adjectives, irregular
- ☐ The formation of adverbs
- ☐ The comparison of adverbs

5. Pronouns

- ☐ Personal: egŏ, tū, nōs and vōs
- ☐ Demonstrative: hic, haec, hoc
- ☐ Demonstrative: is, ea, id
- ☐ Demonstrative: ille, illa, illud
- ☐ Relative: quī, quae, quod
- ☐ Intensive: ipse, ipsa, ipsum
- ☐ Definitive: īdem, eadem, idem

6. Numerals

- ☐ Cardinals 1–20
- ☐ Cardinals 21–1000
- ☐ Ordinals 1st–10th
- ☐ Ordinals 11th–20th

Rules for translating

- ☐ Golden rules (Book I, p. 22)
- ☐ Dealing with the simple past (Book I, p. 42)
- ☐ Agreement of adjectives (Book I, p. 46)
- ☐ Direct questions (Book I, p. 58)
- ☐ The historic present (Book I, p. 60)
- ☐ Breaking up inverted commas (Book I, p. 66)
- ☐ Apposition (Book I, p. 76)
- ☐ Linking sentences and clauses (Book I, p. 82)
- ☐ Translating "and not" and "but not" (Book I, p. 84)
- ☐ Sum plus complement (Book I, p. 88)
- ☐ Dum plus the historic present (Book II, p. 10)
- ☐ Translating "his", "her", "its" and "their" (Book II, p. 16)
- ☐ Transitive and intransitive verbs (Book II, p. 16)
- ☐ Towns, small islands, domus and rūs (Book II, p. 26)
- ☐ Expressions of time (Book II, p. 28)
- ☐ Agents and instruments (Book II, p. 34)
- ☐ Fancy tricks with the P.P.P. (Book II, p. 44)
- ☐ Roman dates (Book II, p. 52)
- ☐ Relative clauses (Book II, p. 56-8)
- ☐ Intransitive verbs in the passive (Book II, p. 75)
- ☐ Translating "can" (Book II, p. 84)

SUMMARY OF GRAMMAR

Verbs: active

Present: I love, I am loving, I do love

amō	moneō	regō	audiō	capiō
amās	monēs	regis	audīs	capis
amat	monet	regit	audit	capit
amāmus	monēmus	regimus	audīmus	capimus
amātis	monētis	regitis	audītis	capitis
amant	monent	regunt	audiunt	capiunt

Future: I shall/will love

amābō	monēbō	regam	audiam	capiam
amābis	monēbis	regēs	audiēs	capiēs
amābit	monēbit	reget	audiet	capiet
amābimus	monēbimus	regēmus	audiēmus	capiēmus
amābitis	monēbitis	regētis	audiētis	capiētis
amābunt	monēbunt	regent	audient	capient

Imperfect: I was loving, I loved, I used to love

amābam	monēbam	regēbam	audiēbam	capiēbam
amābās	monēbās	regēbās	audiēbās	capiēbās
amābat	monēbat	regēbat	audiēbat	capiēbat
amābāmus	monēbāmus	regēbāmus	audiēbāmus	capiēbāmus
amābātis	monēbātis	regēbātis	audiēbātis	capiēbātis
amābant	monēbant	regēbant	audiēbant	capiēbant

Perfect: I have loved, I loved

amāvī	monuī	rēxī	audīvī	cēpī
amāvistī	monuistī	rēxistī	audīvistī	cēpistī
amāvit	monuit	rēxit	audīvit	cēpit
amāvimus	monuimus	rēximus	audīvimus	cēpimus
amāvistis	monuistis	rēxistis	audīvistis	cēpistis
amāvērunt	monuērunt	rēxērunt	audīvērunt	cēpērunt

Future perfect: I shall/will have loved

amāverō	monuerō	rēxerō	audīverō	cēperō
amāveris	monueris	rēxeris	audīveris	cēperis
amāverit	monuerit	rēxerit	audīverit	cēperit
amāverimus	monuerimus	rēxerimus	audīverimus	cēperimus
amāveritis	monueritis	rēxeritis	audīveritis	cēperitis
amāverint	monuerint	rēxerint	audīverint	cēperint

Pluperfect: I had loved

amāveram	monueram	rēxeram	audīveram	cēperam
amāverās	monuerās	rēxerās	audīverās	cēperās
amāverat	monuerat	rēxerat	audīverat	cēperat
amāverāmus	monuerāmus	rēxerāmus	audīverāmus	cēperāmus
amāverātis	monuerātis	rēxerātis	audīverātis	cēperātis
amāverant	monuerant	rēxerant	audīverant	cēperant

Present infinitive: To love

amāre	monēre	regere	audīre	capere

Present imperative: Love!

amā/amāte	monē/monēte	rege/regite	audī/audīte	cape/capite

Verbs: passive

Present: I am loved, I am being loved

amor	moneor	regor	audior	capior
amāris	monēris	regeris	audīris	caperis
amātur	monētur	regitur	audītur	capitur
amāmur	monēmur	regimur	audīmur	capimur
amāminī	monēminī	regiminī	audīminī	capiminī
amantur	monentur	reguntur	audiuntur	capiuntur

Future: I shall/will be loved

amābor	monēbor	regar	audiar	capiar
amāberis	monēberis	regēris	audiēris	capiēris
amābitur	monēbitur	regētur	audiētur	capiētur
amābimur	monēbimur	regēmur	audiēmur	capiēmur
amābiminī	monēbiminī	regēminī	audiēminī	capiēminī
amābuntur	monēbuntur	regentur	audientur	capientur

Imperfect: I was being loved, I was loved, I used to be loved

amābar	monēbar	regēbar	audiēbar	capiēbar
amābāris	monēbāris	regēbāris	audiēbāris	capiēbāris
amābātur	monēbātur	regēbātur	audiēbātur	capiēbātur
amābāmur	monēbāmur	regēbāmur	audiēbāmur	capiēbāmur
amābāminī	monēbāminī	regēbāminī	audiēbāminī	capiēbāminī
amābantur	monēbantur	regēbantur	audiēbantur	capiēbantur

Perfect: I have been loved, I was loved

amātus sum	monitus sum	rēctus sum	audītus sum	captus sum
amātus es	monitus es	rēctus es	audītus es	captus es
amātus est	monitus est	rēctus est	audītus est	captus est
amātī sumus	monitī sumus	rēctī sumus	audītī sumus	captī sumus
amātī estis	monitī estis	rēctī estis	audītī estis	captī estis
amātī sunt	monitī sunt	rēctī sunt	audītī sunt	captī sunt

Future perfect: I shall/will have been loved

amātus erō	monitus erō	rēctus erō	audītus erō	captus erō
amātus eris	monitus eris	rēctus eris	audītus eris	captus eris
amātus erit	monitus erit	rēctus erit	audītus erit	captus erit
amātī erimus	monitī erimus	rēctī erimus	audītī erimus	captī erimus
amātī eritis	monitī eritis	rēctī eritis	audītī eritis	captī eritis
amātī erunt	monitī erunt	rēctī erunt	audītī erunt	captī erunt

Pluperfect: I had been loved

amātus eram	monitus eram	rēctus eram	audītus eram	captus eram
amātus erās	monitus erās	rēctus erās	audītus erās	captus erās
amātus erat	monitus erat	rēctus erat	audītus erat	captus erat
amātī erāmus	monitī erāmus	rēctī erāmus	audītī erāmus	captī erāmus
amātī erātis	monitī erātis	rēctī erātis	audītī erātis	captī erātis
amātī erant	monitī erant	rēctī erant	audītī erant	captī erant

Present infinitive: To be loved

amārī	monērī	regī	audīrī	capī

Present imperative: Be loved!

amāre/amāminī	monēre/monēminī	regere/regiminī	audīre/audīminī	capere/capiminī

Irregular verbs

Present

			Active	Passive
sum	possum	eō	ferō	feror
es	potes	īs	fers	ferris
est	potest	it	fert	fertur
sumus	possumus	īmus	ferimus	ferimur
estis	potestis	ītis	fertis	feriminī
sunt	possunt	eunt	ferunt	feruntur

Future

erō	poterō	ībō	feram	ferar
eris	poteris	ībis	ferēs	ferēris
erit	poterit	ībit	feret	ferētur
erimus	poterimus	ībimus	ferēmus	ferēmur
eritis	poteritis	ībitis	ferētis	ferēminī
erunt	poterunt	ībunt	ferent	ferentur

Imperfect

eram	poteram	ībam	ferēbam	ferēbar
erās	poterās	ībās	ferēbās	ferēbāris
erat	poterat	ībat	ferēbat	ferēbātur
erāmus	poterāmus	ībāmus	ferēbāmus	ferēbāmur
erātis	poterātis	ībātis	ferēbātis	ferēbāminī
erant	poterant	ībant	ferēbant	ferēbantur

Perfect

fuī	potuī	iī	tulī	lātus sum
fuistī	potuistī	īstī	tulistī	lātus es
fuit	potuit	iit	tulit	lātus est
fuimus	potuimus	iimus	tulimus	lātī sumus
fuistis	potuistis	īstis	tulistis	lātī estis
fuērunt	potuērunt	iērunt	tulērunt	lātī sung

Present infinitive

esse	posse	īre	ferre	ferrī

Present imperative

es/este	–	ī/īte	fer/ferte	ferre/feriminī

Nouns

1st declension

Nominative	mēnsa	Table (subject)
Vocative	mēnsa	O table
Accusative	mēnsam	Table (object)
Genitive	mēnsae	Of a table
Dative	mēnsae	To, for a table
Ablative	mēnsā	With, by or from a table

Nominative	mēnsae	Tables (subject)
Vocative	mēnsae	O tables
Accusative	mēnsās	Tables (object)
Genitive	mēnsārum	Of the tables
Dative	mēnsīs	To, for the tables
Ablative	mēnsīs	With, by or from the tables

2nd declension

Nominative	annus	puer	magister	bellum
Vocative	anne	puer	magister	bellum
Accusative	annum	puerum	magistrum	bellum
Genitive	annī	puerī	magistrī	bellī
Dative	annō	puerō	magistrō	bellō
Ablative	annō	puerō	magistrō	bellō

Nominative	annī	puerī	magistrī	bella
Vocative	annī	puerī	magistrī	bella
Accusative	annōs	puerōs	magistrōs	bella
Genitive	annōrum	puerōrum	magistrōrum	bellōrum
Dative	annīs	puerīs	magistrīs	bellīs
Ablative	annīs	puerīs	magistrīs	bellīs

2nd declension, irregular

Nominative	fīlius	deus	vir
Vocative	fīlī	deus	vir
Accusative	fīlium	deum	virum
Genitive	fīlī (fīliī)	deī	virī
Dative	fīliō	deō	virō
Ablative	fīliō	deō	virō

Nominative	fīliī	dī	virī
Vocative	fīliī	dī	virī
Accusative	fīliōs	deōs	virōs
Genitive	fīliōrum	deōrum (deum)	virōrum (virum)
Dative	fīliīs	dīs	virīs
Ablative	fīliīs	dīs	virīs

Nouns (cont.)

3rd declension

Nominative	rēx	opus	cīvis	cubīle
Vocative	rēx	opus	cīvis	cubīle
Accusative	rēgem	opus	cīvem	cubīle
Genitive	rēgis	operis	cīvis	cubīlis
Dative	rēgī	operī	cīvī	cubīlī
Ablative	rēge	opere	cīve	cubīlī

Nominative	rēgēs	opera	cīvēs	cubīlia
Vocative	rēgēs	opera	cīvēs	cubīlia
Accusative	rēgēs	opera	cīvēs	cubīlia
Genitive	rēgum	operum	cīvium	cubīlium
Dative	rēgibus	operibus	cīvibus	cubīlibus
Ablative	rēgibus	operibus	cīvibus	cubīlibus

4th declension

Nominative	gradus	genū	domus
Vocative	gradus	genū	domus
Accusative	gradum	genū	domum
Genitive	gradūs	genūs	domūs
Dative	graduī	genū	domuī (domō)
Ablative	gradū	genū	domō

Nominative	gradūs	genua	domūs
Vocative	gradūs	genua	domūs
Accusative	gradūs	genua	domōs (domūs)
Genitive	graduum	genuum	domuum (domōrum)
Dative	gradibus	genibus	domibus
Ablative	gradibus	genibus	domibus

5th declension

Nominative	rēs	diēs
Vocative	rēs	diēs
Accusative	rem	diem
Genitive	reī	diēī
Dative	reī	diēī
Ablative	rē	diē

Nominative	rēs	diēs
Vocative	rēs	diēs
Accusative	rēs	diēs
Genitive	rērum	diērum
Dative	rēbus	diēbus
Ablative	rēbus	diēbus

Adjectives
1st / 2nd declension

	M	F	N
Nominative	bonus	bona	bonum
Vocative	bone	bona	bonum
Accusative	bonum	bonam	bonum
Genitive	bonī	bonae	bonī
Dative	bonō	bonae	bonō
Ablative	bonō	bonā	bonō

	M	F	N
Nominative	bonī	bonae	bona
Vocative	bonī	bonae	bona
Accusative	bonōs	bonās	bona
Genitive	bonōrum	bonārum	bonōrum
Dative	bonīs	bonīs	bonīs
Ablative	bonīs	bonīs	bonīs

	M	F	N	M	F	N
Nominative	tener	tenera	tenerum	pulcher	pulchra	pulchrum
Vocative	tener	tenera	tenerum	pulcher	pulchra	pulchrum
Accusative	tenerum	teneram	tenerum	pulchrum	pulchram	pulchrum
Genitive	tenerī	tenerae	tenerī	pulchrī	pulchrae	pulchrī
Dative	tenerō	tenerae	tenerō	pulchrō	pulchrae	pulchrō
Ablative	tenerō	tenerā	tenerō	pulchrō	pulchrā	pulchrō

	M	F	N	M	F	N
Nominative	tenerī	tenerae	tenera	pulchrī	pulchrae	pulchra
Vocative	tenerī	tenerae	tenera	pulchrī	pulchrae	pulchra
Accusative	tenerōs	tenerās	tenera	pulchrōs	pulchrās	pulchra
Genitive	tenerōrum	tenerārum	tenerōrum	pulchrōrum	pulchrārum	pulchrōrum
Dative	tenerīs	tenerīs	tenerīs	pulchrīs	pulchrīs	pulchrīs
Ablative	tenerīs	tenerīs	tenerīs	pulchrīs	pulchrīs	pulchrīs

3rd declension

	M	F	N	M	F	N
Nominative	ingēns	ingēns	ingēns	trīstis	trīstis	trīste
Vocative	ingēns	ingēns	ingēns	trīstis	trīstis	trīste
Accusative	ingentem	ingentem	ingēns	trīstem	trīstem	trīste
Genitive	ingentis	ingentis	ingentis	trīstis	trīstis	trīstis
Dative	ingentī	ingentī	ingentī	trīstī	trīstī	trīstī
Ablative	ingentī	ingentī	ingentī	trīstī	trīstī	trīstī

	M	F	N	M	F	N
Nominative	ingentēs	ingentēs	ingentia	trīstēs	trīstēs	trīstia
Vocative	ingentēs	ingentēs	ingentia	trīstēs	trīstēs	trīstia
Accusative	ingentēs	ingentēs	ingentia	trīstēs	trīstēs	trīstia
Genitive	ingentium	ingentium	ingentium	trīstium	trīstium	trīstium
Dative	ingentibus	ingentibus	ingentibus	trīstibus	trīstibus	trīstibus
Ablative	ingentibus	ingentibus	ingentibus	trīstibus	trīstibus	trīstibus

Adjectives (continued)

Nominative	ācer	ācris	ācre	melior	melior	melius
Vocative	ācer	ācris	ācre	melior	melior	melius
Accusative	ācrem	ācrem	ācre	meliōrem	meliōrem	melius
Genitive	ācris	ācris	ācris	meliōris	meliōris	meliōris
Dative	ācrī	ācrī	ācrī	meliōrī	meliōrī	meliōrī
Ablative	ācrī	ācrī	ācrī	meliōre	meliōre	meliōre

Nominative	ācrēs	ācrēs	ācria	meliōrēs	meliōrēs	meliora
Vocative	ācrēs	ācrēs	ācria	meliōrēs	meliōrēs	meliora
Accusative	ācrēs	ācrēs	ācria	meliōrēs	meliōrēs	meliora
Genitive	ācrium	ācrium	ācrium	meliōrum	meliōrum	meliōrum
Dative	ācribus	ācribus	ācribus	meliōribus	meliōribus	meliōribus
Ablative	ācribus	ācribus	ācribus	meliōribus	meliōribus	meliōribus

Pronominal Adjectives

	M	F	N	M	F	N
Nom.	alius	alia	aliud	alter	altera	alterum
Acc.	alium	aliam	aliud	alterum	alteram	alterum
Gen.	alĭus*	alĭus*	alĭus*	alterĭus	alterĭus	alterĭus
Dat.	aliī**	aliī**	aliī**	alterī	alterī	alterī
Abl.	aliō	aliā	aliō	alterō	alterā	alterō

	M	F	N	M	F	N
Nom.	aliī	aliae	alia	alterī	alterae	altera
Acc.	aliōs	aliās	alia	alterōs	alterās	altera
Gen.	aliōrum	aliārum	aliōrum	alterōrum	alterārum	alterōrum
Dat.	aliīs	aliīs	aliīs	alterīs	alterīs	alterīs
Abl.	aliīs	aliīs	aliīs	alterīs	alterīs	alterīs

* alterĭus, the genitive singular of alter, is normally used in place of alĭus.

** alterī, the dative singular of alter, is normally used in place of aliī.

Cardinal Numerals

1	I	ūnus	11	XI	ūndecim	30	XXX	trīgintā
2	II	duŏ	12	XII	duodecim	40	XL	quadrāgintā
3	III	trēs	13	XIII	tredecim	50	L	quīnquāgintā
4	IV/IIII	quattuor	14	XIV	quattuordecim	60	LX	sexāgintā
5	V	quīnque	15	XV	quīndecim	70	LXX	septuāgintā
6	VI	sex	16	XVI	sēdecim	80	LXXX	octōgintā
7	VII	septem	17	XVII	septendecim	90	XC	nōnāgintā
8	VIII	octŏ	18	XVIII	duodēvīgintī	100	C	centum
9	IX	novem	19	XIX	ūndēvīgintī	500	D	quīngentī
10	X	decem	20	XX	vīgintī	1000	M	mīlle

Ordinals

1st	prīmus	11th	ūndecimus
2nd	secundus	12th	duodecimus
3rd	tertius	13th	tertius decimus
4th	quārtus	14th	quārtus decimus
5th	quīntus	15th	quīntus decimus
6th	sextus	16th	sextus decimus
7th	septimus	17th	septimus decimus
8th	octāvus	18th	duodēvīcē(n)simus
9th	nōnus	19th	ūndēvīcē(n)simus
10th	decimus	20th	vīcē(n)simus

Declension of Numerals

	Singular Masc.	Fem.	Neut.	Plural Masc.	Fem.	Neut.
Nom.	ūnus	ūna	ūnum	ūnī	ūnae	ūna
Acc.	ūnum	ūnam	ūnum	ūnōs	ūnās	ūna
Gen.	ūnĭus	ūnĭus	ūnĭus	ūnōrum	ūnārum	ūnōrum
Dat.	ūnī	ūnī	ūnī	ūnīs	ūnīs	ūnīs
Abl.	ūnō	ūnā	ūnō	ūnīs	ūnīs	ūnīs

	Plural Masc.	Fem.	Neut.	Masc.	Plural Fem.	Neut.
Nom.	duŏ	duae	duŏ	trēs	trēs	tria
Acc.	duōs/duŏ	duās	duŏ	trēs	trēs	tria
Gen.	duōrum	duārum	duōrum	trium	trium	trium
Dat.	duōbus	duābus	duōbus	tribus	tribus	tribus
Abl.	duōbus	duābus	duōbus	tribus	tribus	tribus

Pronouns

Personal

Nominative	egŏ	tū	nōs	vōs
Vocative	-	tū	-	vōs
Accusative	mē	tē	nōs	vōs
Genitive	meī	tuī	nostrum/ nostrī *	vestrum/ vestrī *
Dative	mihĭ	tibĭ	nōbīs	vōbīs
Ablative	mē	tē	nōbīs	vōbīs

* Nostrum and vestrum are said to be **partitive genitives**, because they are used after words which express a part (e.g. ūnus nostrum = one of us). Nostrī and vestrī are **objective genitives**, used after nouns and adjectives in which a verbal notion is prominent (e.g. love of us = amor nostrī).

Demonstrative

	M	F	N	M	F	N
Nominative	is	ea	id	ille	illa	illud
Accusative	eum	eam	id	illum	illam	illud
Genitive	eius	eius	eius	illĭus	illĭus	illĭus
Dative	eī	eī	eī	illī	illī	illī
Ablative	eō	eā	eō	illō	illā	illō

	M	F	N	M	F	N
Nominative	eī/iī	eae	ea	illī	illae	illa
Accusative	eōs	eās	ea	illōs	illās	illa
Genitive	eōrum	eārum	eōrum	illōrum	illārum	illōrum
Dative	eīs/iīs	eīs/iīs	eīs/iīs	illīs	illīs	illīs
Ablative	eīs/iīs	eīs/iīs	eīs/iīs	illīs	illīs	illīs

Demonstrative · Relative

	M	F	N	M	F	N
Nominative	hic	haec	hoc	quī	quae	quod
Accusative	hunc	hanc	hoc	quem	quam	quod
Genitive	huius	huius	huius	cuius	cuius	cuius
Dative	huic	huic	huic	cui	cui	cui
Ablative	hōc	hāc	hōc	quō	quā	quō

	M	F	N	M	F	N
Nominative	hī	hae	haec	quī	quae	quae
Accusative	hōs	hās	haec	quōs	quās	quae
Genitive	hōrum	hārum	hōrum	quōrum	quārum	quōrum
Dative	hīs	hīs	hīs	quibus*	quibus*	quibus*
Ablative	hīs	hīs	hīs	quibus*	quibus*	quibus*

*or quīs

Pronouns (continued)

Intensive

	M	F	N
Nominative	ipse	ipsa	ipsum
Accusative	ipsum	ipsam	ipsum
Genitive	ipsĭus	ipsĭus	ipsĭus
Dative	ipsī	ipsī	ipsī
Ablative	ipsō	ipsā	ipsō

	M	F	N
Nominative	ipsī	ipsae	ipsa
Accusative	ipsōs	ipsās	ipsa
Genitive	ipsōrum	ipsārum	ipsōrum
Dative	ipsīs	ipsīs	ipsīs
Ablative	ipsīs	ipsīs	ipsīs

Definitive

	M	F	N
Nominative	īdem	eadem	ĭdem
Accusative	eundem	eandem	ĭdem
Genitive	eiusdem	eiusdem	eiusdem
Dative	eīdem	eīdem	eīdem
Ablative	eōdem	eādem	eōdem

	M	F	N
Nominative	eīdem/īdem	eaedem	eadem
Accusative	eōsdem	eāsdem	eadem
Genitive	eōrundem	eārundem	eōrundem
Dative	eīsdem*	eīsdem*	eīsdem*
Ablative	eīsdem*	eīsdem*	eīsdem*

* or īsdem

APPENDIX

More on vowel quantity

It is a brave man who inserts a macron over a vowel in a book which is to be read by people outside his immediate family. Or chooses not to do so, for that matter. Just think of the hoots of derision that will be heard, ringing through the countryside, as the errors are spotted and chortled over.

Well, just to make clear what I have done, or attempted to do, here are a few notes. I am for ever in debt to Theo Zinn, with whom I defy anyone to argue on matters of quantity. Theo taught me everything I know and many a happy hour has been spent in his company, looking up obscure references in search of the answers to some of the more niggling problems of Latin vowel quantity, but no doubt you will all have your own views on my decisions.

1. Vowels are marked as long where they are known to be long.
2. Vowels are sometimes marked as short where the tendency to get them wrong is so distressing as to require correction (thus egŏ).
3. Vowels are marked as anceps (= ambiguous) where the vowel could be pronounced either long or short as, for example, in: octŏ, homŏ, quandŏ, ibĭ and ubĭ.
4. Consonant i: Both Allen (Vox Latina, p. 38-9) and Kennedy (Revised Latin Primer, p. 42, note 3) agree that consonant i between two vowels in words such as huius and eius was pronounced as a doubled consonant and thus that while the preceding vowel was short, the syllable always *scans* long. Books which thus *mark* words such as maior, peior, Troia, etc. as having a long first syllable are presumably doing so for the benefit of pupils writing or scanning verse. But if macrons are there principally to aid pronunciation, as in a book of this sort, they are clearly most misleading if inserted over what are in fact agreed to be short vowels. Note that, in the name Gāĭus, the ĭ is a vowel, not a consonant, and the ā really is long!
5. No attempt has been made to indicate whether the letters i and u are vowels or consonants. It seems sad that the practice of writing consonant *i* as a j has been abandoned but it has, so there we go. As for u, how one was ever supposed to know that, in a word such as persuādeō, there was a "w"sound rather than a "u" sound, goodness only knows.
6. Vowels before ns and nf are always long, even (as Allen tells us, p. 65, note 2) at word junction. Thus the need to mark the i of īn sitū, for example, as long.
7. Latin words which have become, by adoption, English ones have caused me some difficulty in the *Using Latin* boxes. I have had to decide whether to write a word such as *alias* as a Latin word, with macrons where appropriate, or as an English one (and thus with no macrons). My policy here, such as it is, has been always to give the Latin word at the top, correctly marked, but to show the word unmarked in the explanation where it has become so much a part of the English language as to have lost its Latin quality altogether. Such words as *via*, *alibi* and *extra* would fit into this category, whereas phrases such as status quō would not.
8. The ui of cui and huic is a dipthong and is thus not marked with a macron. When pronouncing these words, remember that they are one-syllable words, not two.

LATIN – ENGLISH VOCABULARY

(Including all words used in Books I and II, together with some additional, commonly-used words)

ā, ab + abl. = by, from

abhinc = ago

absum, abesse, āfuī = I am absent

ac (not before a vowel or h) = and

accūsō, -āre, -āvī, -ātum = I accuse

āctus: *see* **agō**

ad + acc. = to, towards

adeō, adīre, adiī, aditum = I approach

adfuī: *see* **adsum**

adiuvō, -āre, adiūvī, adiūtum = I help

adsum, adesse, adfuī = I am present

adveniō, -īre, advēnī, adventum = I arrive

aedificō, -āre, -āvī, -ātum = I build

aestās, -ātis, f. = summer

āfuī: *see* **absum**

ager, agrī, m. = field

aggredior, aggredī, aggressus sum = I attack

agō, agere, ēgī, āctum = I do

agricola, -ae, m. = farmer

aliēnus, -a, -um = of another, belonging to another

aliās (adverb) = at another time

alius, alia, aliud = other

alloquor, alloquī, allocūtus sum = I address

alter, altera, alterum = the other (of two)

altus, -a, -um = deep, high

ambulō, -āre, -āvī, -ātum = I walk

amīcus, -ī, m. = friend

amō, amāre, amāvī, amātum = I love, like

animal, animālis, n. = animal

animus, -ī, m. = mind, spirit

annus, -ī, m. = year

ānser, ānseris, m. = goose

ante + acc. = before

ante (adverb) = before

antequam (conjunction) = before

aperiō, -īre, aperuī, apertum = I open

appellō, -āre, -āvī, -ātum = I call

appropinquō, -āre, -āvī, -ātum = I approach

apud + acc. = at the house of, among, at, near

aqua, -ae, f. = water

arbor, -ŏris, f. = tree

argentum, -ī, n. = silver, money

arma, -ōrum, n. pl. = weapons

ars, artis, f. = skill, art

arx, arcis, f. = citadel

ascendō, -ere, ascendī, ascēnsum = I climb

atque = and

ātrium, ātriī, n. = hall

audācter (adverb) = boldly

audāx, audācis = bold

audeō, audēre, ausus sum = I dare

audiō, -īre, -īvī, -ītum = I hear, listen to

aurum, -ī, n. = gold

ausus: *see* **audeō**

autem = however, moreover (never first word in clause)

auxilium, -iī, n. = help

barbarus, -a, -um = barbarian (adjective)

barbarus, -ī, m. = barbarian (noun)

bellum, -ī, n. = war

bene (adverb) = well

bibō, -ere, bibī = I drink

bonus, -a, -um = good

brevis, breve = short, brief

cadō, -ere, cecidī, cāsum = I fall

caelum, -ī, n. = sky

campus, -ī, m. = plain

canis, canis, c. = dog

cantō, -āre, -āvī, -ātum = I sing

capiō, -ere, cēpī, captum = I take, capture

captīvus, -ī, m. = prisoner

captus: *see* capiō
caput, -itis, n. = head
carmen, carminis, n. = poem, song
cārus, -a, -um = dear
castra pōnō = I pitch a camp
castra, -ōrum, n. pl. = camp
cecidī: *see* cadō
celer, celeris, celere = swift, quick
celeriter (adverb) = quickly
cēlō, -āre, -āvī, -ātum = I hide
cēna, -ae, f. = dinner
cēnō, -āre, -āvī, -ātum = I dine
centum = one hundred
cēpī: *see* capiō
cēterī, -ae, -a = other, remaining, the rest
cibus, -ī, m. = food
circum + acc. = around
cīvis, cīvis, c. = citizen
clāmō, -āre, -āvī, -ātum = I shout
clāmor, -ōris, m. = shout
clārus, -a, -um = famous
classis, classis, f. = fleet
claudō, claudere, clausī, clausum =
    I close
coāctum: *see* cōgō
coēgī: *see* cōgō
cognōscō, -ere, cognōvī, cognitum =
    I learn, find out
cōgō, cōgere, coēgī, coāctum =
    I compel, force
collis, collis, m. = hill
comes, comitis, c. = companion
cōnficiō, -ere, cōnfēcī, cōnfectum =
    I complete
cōnor, cōnārī, cōnātus sum = I try
cōnsilium capiō = I adopt a plan
cōnsilium, -iī, n. = plan
cōnstituō, -ere, cōnstituī,
    cōnstitūtum = I decide
cōnsul, cōnsulis, m. = consul
contendō, contendere, contendī,
    contentum = I hurry, march, strive
contrā + acc. = against
conveniō, -īre, convēnī, conventum =
    I come together

cōpiae, -ārum, f. pl. = forces
cornū, -ūs, n. = horn, wing (of an army)
corpus, -ŏris, n. = body
cōtīdiē = every day
crās = tomorrow
crēdō, -ere, crēdidī, crēditum + dat. =
    I trust, believe
crūdēlis, -e = cruel
cubīle, cubīlis, n. = bed
cucurrī: *see* currō
cum + abl. = with, together with
cupiō, -ere, -īvī, -ītum = I want, desire
cūr? = why?
cūra, -ae, f. = care
cūrō, -āre, -āvī, -ātum = I care for
currō, -ere, cucurrī, cursum = I run
custōs, custōdis, c. = guard
datus: *see* dō
dē + abl. = down from, concerning
dea, -ae, f. = goddess (dat. and abl. pl. =
    deābus)
dēbeō, -ēre, -uī, -itum = I ought, owe
decem = ten
dedī: *see* dō
dēfendō, -ere, dēfendī, dēfēnsum =
    I defend
deinde = then
dēlectō, -āre, -āvī, -ātum = I delight,
    please
dēleō, dēlēre, dēlēvī, dēlētum =
    I destroy
dēscendō, -ere, dēscendī,
    dēscēnsum = I go down
dēspērō, -āre, -āvī, -ātum =
    I despair
deus, deī, m. (irreg.) = god
dexter, dextra, dextrum = right (as
    opposed to "left")
dīcō, dīcere, dīxī, dictum = I say
didicī: *see* discō
diēs, diēī, m. = day (fem. if an
    appointed day)
difficilis, -e = difficult
dignus, -a, -um + abl. = worthy (of)
dīligēns, -entis = careful

discēdō, -ere, discessī, discessum = I depart

discō, -ere, didicī = I learn

diū (adverb) = for a long time

diūtissimē (adverb) = for a very long time

diūtius (adverb) = longer (of time)

dīxī: *see* dīcō

dō, dăre, dedī, dătum = I give

doceō, -ēre, docuī, doctum = I teach

doleō, -ēre, doluī, dolitum = I feel pain, am sad

dolor, dolōris, m. = pain, grief

dominus, -ī, m. = master, lord

domus, -ūs, f. (irreg.) = house, home

dōnum, -ī, n. = gift

dormiō, -īre, -īvī, -ītum = I sleep

dūcō, -ere, dūxī, ductum = I lead

dulcis, -e = charming, pleasant

dum = while

duŏ = two

duodecim = twelve

duodēvīgintī = eighteen

dūrus, -a, -um = hard

dux, ducis, c. = leader

ē, ex + abl. = out of

eadem: *see* īdem

ecce = look!

effugiō, -ere, effūgī = I escape

ēgī: *see* agō

egŏ = I

ēgredior, ēgredī, ēgressus sum = I go out

enim = for (never written first word)

eō = to that place (thither)

eō, īre, iī (*or* īvī), itum (irreg.) = I go

epistola (*or* epistula), -ae, f. = letter

eques, equitis, m. = horseman (pl. = cavalry)

equus, equī, m. = horse

ergŏ = therefore

errō, -āre, -āvī, -ātum = I wander

esse: *see* sum

et = and

et...et = both...and

etiam = even, also

ex + abl. = out of

exeō, exīre, exiī, exitum = I go out

exercitus, -ūs, m. = army

exspectō, -āre, -āvī, -ātum = I wait for

extrā + acc. = outside

fābula, -ae, f. = story

facile (adverb) = easily

facilis, -e = easy

faciō, -ere, fēcī, factum = I do, make

fāma, -ae, f. = fame, glory

fēcī: *see* faciō

fēlīciter (adverb) = fortunately, favourably

fēlīx, fēlīcis = fortunate, favourable, happy

fēmina, -ae, f. = woman

ferō, ferre, tulī, lātum (irreg.) = I carry, bear, (of roads = I lead)

fessus, -a, -um = tired

festīnō, -āre, -āvī, -ātum = I hurry

fidēlis, -e = faithful

fidēliter (adverb) = faithfully

fīlia, -ae, f. = daughter (dat. and abl. pl. = fīliābus)

fīlius, fīliī (*or* fīlī), m. (irreg.) = son

fīnis, -is, m. = end (pl. = territory)

fleō, flēre, flēvī, flētum = I weep

flōs, flōris, m. = flower

flūmen, flūminis, n. = river

fōns, fontis, m. = fountain

fortasse = perhaps

forte = by chance

fortis, -e = brave, strong

fortiter (adverb) = bravely

fōrtūna, -ae, f. = fortune

forum, -ī, n. = forum

frangō, -ere, frēgī, frāctum = I break

frāter, frātris, m. = brother

frēgī: *see* frangō

frūstrā = in vain

fuga, -ae, f. = flight, escape

fugiō, -ere, fūgī = I flee

fuī: *see* sum

Gallia, -ae, f. = Gaul (the country)
Gallus, -ī, m. = a Gaul (the person)
gaudeō, gaudēre, gāvīsus sum =
    I rejoice
gaudium, gaudiī, n. = joy
gēns, gentis, f. = people, race,
genū, genūs, n. = knee
gerō, -ere, gessī, gestum = I manage,
    wage (a war), wear
gessī: *see* **gerō**
gladius, gladiī, m. = sword
gradus, gradūs, m. = step
Graecia, -ae, f. = Greece
grātiās agō = I give thanks
gravis, -e = heavy, serious
habeō, -ēre -uī, -itum = I have
habitō, -āre, -āvī, -ātum = I live,
    inhabit
hasta, -ae, f. = spear
herba, -ae, f. = grass
herī = yesterday
hīc = here
hic, haec, hoc = this; he, she, it
hinc = from here, hence
hodiē = today
homŏ, hominis, c. = man, person
hōra, -ae, f. = hour
hortor, -ārī, hortātus sum =
    I encourage, urge
hortus, -ī, m. = garden
hostis, hostis, c. = enemy (usually used
    in plural)
hūc = to here, hither
iaceō, -ēre, iacuī, iacitum = I lie
    (down)
iaciō, -ere, iēcī, iactum = I throw
iam = now, already
ibĭ = there
īdem, eadem, idem = the same
iēcī: *see* **iaciō**
igitur = therefore (never written first
    word)
ignis, ignis, m. = fire
iī: *see* **eō**
ille, illa, illud = that; he, she, it

illīc = there
illinc = from there, thence
illūc = to there, thither
imperātor, -ōris, m. = general
imperium, -iī, n. = command, empire
in + abl. = in, on
in + acc. = into, on to
incendium, -iī, n. = fire
incendō, -ere, incendī, incēnsum =
    I burn, set alight
incipiō, -ere, incēpī, inceptum =
    I begin
incola, -ae, c. = inhabitant
inde = then
ineō, -īre, iniī, initum = I go in
ingenium, -iī, n. = ability
ingēns, ingentis = huge
ingredior, ingredī, ingressus sum =
    I go in
inimīcus, -ī, m. = (private) enemy
inquit = he/she says
inquiunt = they say
īnsula, -ae, f. = island
intellegō, -ere, intellēxī, intellēctum =
    I understand
inter + acc. = between, among
intereā = meanwhile
interficiō, -ere, interfēcī, interfectum
    = I kill
intrā + acc. = within
intrō, -āre, -āvī, -ātum = I enter
inveniō, -īre, invēnī, inventum = I find
ipse, ipsa, ipsum = self
īra, -ae, f. = anger
īrāscor, īrāscī, īrātus sum (+ dat. of
    thing or person) = I am angry
īrātus, -a, -um = angry
īre: *see* **eō**
is, ea, id = that; he, she, it
ita = thus
Ītalia, -ae, f. = Italy
itaque = therefore
iter, itineris, n. = journey
iter faciō = I make a journey, travel
iterum = again

iubeō, -ēre, iussī, iussum = I order
iūdex, iūdicis, c. = judge
Iuppiter, Iovis, m. = Jupiter
iussus: *see* iubeō
iuvenis, iuvenis, c. = young person
   (normally = "young man")
iuvō, iuvāre, iūvī, iūtum = I help
īvī: *see* eō
labor, labōris, m. = work, task
labōrō, -āre, -āvī, -ātum = I work
lacrima, -ae, f. = tear
laetus, -a, -um = happy
lātus: *see* ferō
laudō, -āre, -āvī, -ātum = I praise
lēctus: *see* legō
lēgātus, -ī, m. = ambassador
legiō, -ōnis, f. = legion
legō, -ere, lēgī, lēctum = I read, choose
lentē = slowly
leō, leōnis, m. = lion
lēx, lēgis, f. = law
līber, -era, -erum = free
liber, librī, m. = book
līberī, -ōrum, m. pl. = offspring, sons
   and daughters, children (i.e. in
   relation to their parents)
līberō, -āre, -āvī, -ātum = I free
littera, -ae, f. = letter (of the alphabet);
   in plural = a letter (which you send
   to someone), literature
locus, -ī, m. = place (plural = loca,
   -ōrum, n. pl., when this refers to a
   region as opposed to single places)
locūtus: *see* loquor
longus, -a, -um = long
loquor, loquī, locūtus sum = I speak
lūdō, -ere, lūsī, lūsum = I play
lūdus, -ī, m. = school
lūna, -ae, f. = moon
lūsī: *see* lūdō
lūx, lūcis, f. = light
magister, magistrī, m. = master,
   school-master
magnopere = greatly
magnus, -a, -um = big, great

maior, maius = bigger, greater
malus, -a, -um = bad
maneō, -ēre, mānsī, mānsum =
   I remain
manus, -ūs, f. = hand, (or "band of men")
mare, maris, n. = sea
māter, mātris, f. = mother
mātrimōnium, -iī, n. = marriage
maximus, -a, -um = biggest, greatest
mē: *see* egō
medius, -a, -um = middle
melior, melius = better
mēnsa, mēnsae, f. = table
meus, -a, -um = my
mihī: *see* egō
mīles, mīlitis, c. = soldier
mīlle = one thousand
minimus, -a, -um = smallest
minor, minus = smaller
mīror, mīrārī, mīrātus sum = I wonder
   at, am amazed at
miser, -era, -erum = wretched
mīsī: *see* mittō
mittō, -ere, mīsī, missum = I send
modus, -ī, m. = way, manner
moneō, -ēre, -uī, -itum = I warn, advise
mōns, montis, m. = mountain
morior, morī, mortuus sum = I die
moror, morārī, morātus sum = I delay
mors, mortis, f. = death
mortuus, -a, -um = dead
mōs, mōris, m. = custom
moveō, -ēre, mōvī, mōtum = I move,
   i.e. set in motion
mox = soon
mulier, mulieris, f. = woman
multum (adverb) = much, a lot
multus, -a, -um = much, many
mūrus, -ī, m. = wall
nam = for
nārrō, -āre, -āvī, -ātum = I tell
nāscor, nāscī, nātus sum = I am born
nātus, -a, -um = born, old (e.g. x years
   old)
nauta, -ae, m. = sailor

nāvigō, -āre, -āvī, -ātum = I sail
nāvis, nāvis, f. = ship
-ne?: introduces a question
nec = and not, nor
nec tamen = but...not
nec...nec = neither...nor
necō, -āre, -āvī, -ātum = I kill
**nēmŏ, (nēminem, nūllĭus, nēminī,
    nūllō)**, c. = no one
neque = and not, nor
neque tamen = but...not
neque...neque = neither...nor
nesciō, -īre, -īvī, -ītum = I do not know
niger, nigra, nigrum = black
nihil = nothing
nōbīs: *see* **nōs**
noctū = by night, at night
nōmen, nōminis, n. = name
nōn = not
nōn sōlum...sed etiam = not only...but
    also
nōnne?: introduces a question
    (expecting the answer "yes")
nōs = we
noster, nostra, nostrum = our
nōtus, -a, -um = well-known
novem = nine
novus, -a, -um = new
nox, noctis, f. = night
num?: introduces a question (expecting
    the answer "no")
numquam = never
nunc = now
nūntiō, -āre, -āvī, -ātum = I report,
    announce
nūntius, nūntiī, m. = messenger,
    message
occīdō, -ere, occīdī, occīsum = I kill
occupō, -āre, -āvī, -ātum = I seize
octŏ = eight
oculus, -ī, m. = eye
ōlim = once upon a time
omnis, -e = every, all
oppidum, -ī, n. = town
oppugnō, -āre, -āvī, -ātum = I attack

(a city or camp)
optimus, -a, um = best
opus, operis, n. = work
ōra, -ae, f. = shore
ōrātiō, -ōnis, f. = speech
ōrdior, ōrdīrī, ōrsus sum = I begin
orior, orīrī, ortus sum = I arise (mixed
    conjugation)
ōrō, -āre, -āvī, -ātum = I beg, pray
**ostendō, -ere, ostendī, ostēnsum /
    ostentum** = I show
paene = almost
pānis, pānis, m. = bread
parēns, parentis, c. = parent
pāreō, -ēre, -uī, -itum (+ dat.) = I obey
pariō, -ere, peperī, partum = I
    produce, (of victories) I win
parō, -āre, -āvī, -ātum = I prepare
pars, partis, f. = part
partior, -īrī, partītus sum = I share
parvus, -a, -um = small
pater, patris, m. = father
patria, -ae, f. = country, fatherland
paucī, -ae, -a = few
pāx, pācis, f. = peace
pecūnia, -ae, f. = money
pedes, peditis, m. = foot-soldier
peior, peius = worse
pellō, -ere, pepulī, pulsum = I drive
peperī: *see* **pariō**
per + acc. = through, along
pereō, -īre, periī, peritum = I die
perfidia, -ae, f. = treachery
perīculum, -ī, n. = danger
**persuādeō, -ēre, persuāsī,
    persuāsum** (+ dat.) = I persuade
pēs, pedis, m. = foot
pessimus, -a, -um = worst
petō, -ere, petīvī, petītum = I seek,
    make for
plūrimus, -a, -um = most, very many
plūs, plūris = more (neuter noun in
    singular; adjective in plural)
plūs (adverb) = more
Poenī, -ōrum, m. pl. = Carthaginians

poēta, -ae, m. = poet
pōnō, -ere, posuī, positum = I place, pitch (a camp)
pōns, pontis, m. = bridge
populus, -ī, m. = a people, population
porta, -ae, f. = gate
portō, -āre, -āvī, -ātum = I carry
portus, -ūs, m. = harbour
positus: *see* pōnō
possum, posse, potuī (irreg.) = I am able
post + acc. = after
post (adverb) = behind, (of time) afterwards
posteā = afterwards
posterius (adverb) = later
postquam (conjunction) = after
postrēmō (adverb) = finally
posuī: *see* pōnō
potuī: *see* possum
praemium, -iī, n. = reward
pretium, -iī, n. = price
prīma hōra, -ae, f. = the first hour, dawn
prīma lūx, lūcis, f. = first light, dawn
prīmō / prīmum = at first
prīnceps, prīncipis, c. = chief, leader
prō + abl. = on behalf of, in place of
proelium, -iī, n. = battle
proficīscor, proficīscī, profectus sum = I set out
prōgredior, prōgredī, prōgressus sum = I go forward
prōmittō, -ere, prōmīsī, prōmissum = I promise
prope + acc. = near
propter + acc. = on account of
proximē (adverb) = very nearly, (of time) just now
puella, -ae, f. = girl
puer, puerī, m. = boy
pugna, -ae, f. = battle, fight
pugnō, -āre, -āvī, -ātum = I fight
pulcher, -chra, -chrum = beautiful
pulchrē (adverb) = beautifully

pulsus: *see* pellō
Pūnicus, -a, um = Carthaginian
pūniō, -īre, -īvī, -ītum = I punish
putō, -āre, -āvī, -ātum = I think
quaerō, -ere, quaesīvī, quaesītum = I ask, seek
quam = than
quamquam = although
quandŏ? = when?
quattuor = four
quattuordecim = fourteen
-que = and
quī, quae, quod = who, which
quid? = what?
quīndecim = fifteen
quīnque = five
quis? = who?
quod = because
quōmodŏ? = how?
quoque = also
quot? = how many?
rēctus: *see* regō
rēctus, -a, -um = right (as opposed to "wrong")
reddō, reddere, reddidī, redditum = I return, give back
redeō, redīre, rediī, reditum = I go back
redūcō, -ere, redūxī, reductum = I lead back
rēgīna, -ae, f. = queen
regō, -ere, rēxī, rēctum = I rule
regredior, regredī, regressus sum = I go back
relinquō, -ere, relīquī, relictum = I leave
rēs, reī, f. = thing, affair
respondeō, -ēre, respondī, respōnsum = I reply, answer
reveniō, -īre, revēnī, reventum = I come back, return
rēx, rēgis, m. = king
rēxī: *see* regō
rīdeō, -ēre, rīsī, rīsum = I laugh, smile
rīpa, -ae, f. = bank (of a river)

rogō, -āre, -āvī, -ātum = I ask
Rōma, -ae, f. = Rome
Rōmānus, -a, -um = Roman (adjective)
Rōmānus, -ī, m. = Roman (noun)
ruō, ruere, ruī, rutum = I rush
rūs, rūris, n. = the countryside
sacer, sacra, sacrum = sacred
saepe = often
saevus, -a, -um = savage
sagitta, -ae, f. = arrow
salūtō, -āre, -āvī, -ātum = I greet
salvē, salvēte = hello, greetings!
sapiēns, sapientis = wise
sapienter (adverb) = wisely
sapientia, -ae, f. = wisdom
satis = enough
saxum, -ī, n. = rock
sciō, scīre, scīvī, scītum = I know
scrībō, -ere, scrīpsī, scrīptum = I write
scūtum, -ī, n. = shield
sē = himself, herself, itself, themselves
secūtus: *see* **sequor**
sed = but
sēdecim = sixteen
sedeō, sedēre, sēdī, sessum = I sit
semper = always
senex, senis, m. = old man
septem = seven
septendecim = seventeen
sequor, sequī, secūtus sum = I follow
servō, -āre, -āvī, -ātum = I save
servus, -ī, m. = slave
sex = six
sī = if
sīc = thus
signum, -ī, n. = signal, sign
silva, -ae, f. = wood, forest
sine + abl. = without
sinister, -tra, -trum = left, on the left
socius, -iī, m. = ally
sōl, sōlis, m. = sun
sōlus, -a, -um (goes like **ūnus**) = alone
somnium, -iī, n. = dream
somnus, -ī, m. = sleep
soror, -ōris, f. = sister

spectō, -āre, -āvī, -ātum = I watch
statim = immediately
stetī: *see* **stō**
stō, stāre, stetī, stătum = I stand
stultus, -a, -um = stupid
sub + abl. = under
subitō = suddenly
sum, esse, fuī (irreg.) = I am
summus, -a, -um = topmost, top of
super + acc. = over
superbus, -a, -um = proud
superō, -āre, -āvī, -ātum = I overcome, conquer
surgō, -ere, surrēxī, surrēctum = I rise, get up
suus, sua, suum = his (own), her (own), its (own) or their (own)
taberna, -ae, f. = inn, shop
tāctum: *see* **tangō**
tālis, -e = such
tamen = however (not written first word in clause)
tandem = at last
tangō, tangere, tetigī, tāctum = I touch
tantus, -a, -um = so great
tēlum, -ī, n. = spear, missile
tempestās, -ātis, f. = storm, weather
templum, -ī, n. = temple
tempus, -ŏris, n. = time
teneō, -ēre, tenuī, tentum = I hold
tener, -era, -erum = tender
terra, -ae, f. = land, earth
terreō, -ēre, -uī, -itum = I terrify
tetigī: *see* **tangō**
theātrum, -ī, n. = theatre
timeō, -ēre, -uī = I fear
tōtus, -a, -um (goes like **ūnus**) = whole
trādō, -ere, trādidī, trāditum = I hand over
trahō, -ere, traxī, tractum = I drag
trāns + acc. = across
tredecim = thirteen
trēs = three
trīstis, trīste = sad, gloomy

Troia, -ae, f. = Troy

tū = you (singular)

tulī: *see* **ferō**

tum = then, at that time, next

tunc = then, at that time

tūtō (adverb) = safely

tūtus, -a, -um = safe

tuus, -a, -um = your

ubĭ = when; where

ubĭ? = where?

unda, -ae, f. = wave

ūndecim = eleven

ūndēvīgintī = nineteen

ūnus, -a, -um (gen. sing. = **ūnĭus**, dat. sing. = **ūnī**) = one, only one, one alone

urbs, urbis, f. = city

ūtor, ūtī, ūsus sum (+ abl.) = I use

uxor, -ōris, f. = wife

valēns, valentis = strong

validus, -a, -um = strong

veniō, -īre, vēnī, ventum = I come

ventus, -ī, m. = wind

verbum, -ī, n. = word

vereor, verērī, veritus sum = I fear

vertō, -ere, vertī, versum = I turn

vester, vestra, vestrum = your

vestis, vestis, f. = clothing

via, -ae, f. = road, street, way

victōria, -ae, f. = victory

victōriam pariō = I win a victory

videō, -ēre, vīdī, vīsum = I see

videor, vidērī, vīsus sum = I seem

vīgintī = twenty

vīlla, -ae, f. = country house, villa

vincō, -ere, vīcī, victum = I conquer

vir, virī, m. (irreg.) = man

virtūs, virtūtis, f. = courage

vīsus: *see* **videō**

vīta, -ae, f. = life

vītō, -āre, -āvī, -ātum = I avoid

vōbīs: *see* **vōs**

vocō, -āre, -āvī, -ātum = I call

vōs = you (plural)

vōx, vōcis, f. = voice

vulnerō, -āre, -āvī, -ātum = I wound

vulnus, vulneris, n. = wound

ENGLISH – LATIN VOCABULARY
(Including all words used in Books I and II, together with some additional, commonly-used words)

Ability = **ingenium, -iī**, n.
Able, I am = **possum, posse, potuī** (irreg.)
Absent, I am = **absum, abesse, āfuī** (irreg.)
Accuse, I = **accūsō, -āre, -āvī, -ātum**
Across = **trāns** + acc.
Advance, I = **progredior, prōgredī, prōgressus sum**
Advise, I = **moneō, -ēre, -uī, -itum**
Affair, matter = **rēs, reī**, f.
After (conjunction) = **postquam**
After (preposition) = **post** + acc.
After (adverb) = **post**
Afterwards = **posteā**; x years afterwards = **post** with abl., e.g. **duōbus post annīs**
Again = **iterum**
Against = **contrā** + acc.
Ago = **abhinc** + acc. (or abl.)
All = **omnis, -e**
Ally = **socius, -iī**, m.
Almost = **paene**
Alone = **sōlus, -a, -um** (*goes like* **ūnus**)
Alone, only one = **ūnus, -a, -um** (gen. sing. = **ūnĭus**, dat. sing. = **ūnī**)
Already = **iam**
Also = **etiam; quoque**
Although = **quamquam**
Always = **semper**
Am, I = **sum, esse, fuī** (irreg.)
Amazed at, I am = **mīror, mīrārī, mīrātus sum**
Ambassador = **lēgātus, -ī**, m.
Among = **inter** + acc.
And = **et; atque; ac** (not before vowels or **h**)
And...not = **nec; neque**
Anger = **īra, -ae**, f.
Angry = **īrātus, -a, -um**

Angry, I am = **īrāscor, īrāscī, īrātus sum** (+ dat. of thing or person)
Animal = **animal, animālis**, n.
Announce, I = **nūntiō, -āre, -āvī, -ātum**
Answer, I = **respondeō, -ēre, respondī, respōnsum**
Approach, I = **adeō, adīre, adiī, aditum** (*goes like* **eō**); **appropinquō, -āre, -āvī, -ātum**
Arise, I = **orior, orīrī, ortus sum**
Arms (weapons) = **arma, -ōrum**, n. pl.
Army = **exercitus, -ūs**, m.
Around = **circum** + acc.
Arrive, I = **adveniō, -īre, advēnī, adventum**
Arrow = **sagitta, -ae**, f.
Art = **ars, artis**, f.
Ask, I = **rogō, -āre, -āvī, -ātum**
At last = **tandem**
At the house of, among = **apud** + acc.
Attack, I (a city) = **oppugnō, -āre, -āvī, -ātum**; (a person) **aggredior, aggredī, aggressus sum**
Avoid, I = **vītō, -āre, -āvī, -ātum**
Bad = **malus, -a, -um**
Band of men = **manus, -ūs**, f.
Bank (of a river) = **rīpa, -ae**, f.
Barbarian (noun) = **barbarus, -ī**, m.
Barbarian (adjective) = **barbarus, -a, -um**
Battle = **pugna, -ae**, f.; **proelium, -iī**, n.
Bear, I = **ferō, ferre, tulī, lātum** (irreg.)
Beautiful = **pulcher, -chra, -chrum**
Beautifully (adverb) = **pulchrē**
Because = **quod**
Because of = **propter** + acc.
Bed = **cubīle, cubīlis**, n.
Before (conjunction) = **antequam**
Before (preposition) = **ante** + acc.
Before (adverb) = **ante**

Begin, I = **incipiō, -ere, incēpī, inceptum**; *or* use imperfect tense of verb (e.g. amābam = I *began* to love)

Believe, I = **crēdō, -ere, crēdidī, crēditum** + dat.

Best = **optimus, -a, -um**

Better = **melior, -us**

Between = **inter** + acc.

Big = **magnus, -a, -um**

Bigger = **maior, -us**

Biggest = **maximus, -a, -um**

Black = **niger, nigra, nigrum**

Body = **corpus, -ŏris**, n.

Bold = **audāx, audācis**

Boldly (adverb) = **audācter**

Book = **liber, librī**, m.

Born, I am = **nāscor, nāscī, nātus sum**

Both…and = **et…et**

Boy = **puer, puerī**, m.

Brave = **fortis, -e**

Bravely (adverb) = **fortiter**

Bread = **pānis, pānis**, m.

Break, I = **frangō, -ere, frēgī, frāctum**

Bridge = **pōns, pontis**, m.

Brief = **brevis, breve**

Brother = **frāter, frātris**, m.

Build, I = **aedificō, -āre, -āvī, -ātum**

Burn (set alight), I = **incendō, -ere, incendī, incēnsum**

But = **sed**

But…not = **nec tamen; neque tamen**

By = **ā, ab** + abl.

By chance = **forte**

Call (by name), I = **appellō, -āre, -āvī, -ātum**

Call (i.e. cry out), I = **vocō, -āre, -āvī, -ātum**

Camp = **castra, -ōrum**, n. pl.

Can: *use* **possum** + infin.

Capture, I = **capiō, -ere, cēpī, captum**

Care (noun) = **cūra, -ae**, f.

Care for, I = **cūrō, -āre, -āvī, -ātum**

Careful = **dīligēns, -entis**

Carry, I = **portō, -āre, -āvī, -ātum; ferō, ferre, tulī, lātum** (irreg.)

Carthaginian (adjective) = **Pūnicus, -a, -um**

Carthaginians, the = **Poenī, -ōrum**, m. pl.

Cavalry = **equitēs, equitum**, m. pl.

Chief = **prīnceps, prīncipis**, c.

Children (i.e. sons and daughters, offspring) = **līberī, līberōrum**, m. pl.

Choose, I = **legō, -ere, lēgī, lēctum**

Citadel = **arx, arcis**, f.

Citizen = **cīvis, cīvis**, c.

City = **urbs, urbis**, f.

Climb, I = **ascendō, -ere, ascendī, ascēnsum**

Close, I = **claudō, claudere, clausī, clausum**

Clothing = **vestis, vestis**, f.

Come together, I = **conveniō, -īre, convēnī, conventum**

Come, I = **veniō, -īre, vēnī, ventum**

Command (noun) = **imperium, -iī**, n.

Companion = **comes, comitis**, c.

Compel, I = **cōgō, cōgere, coēgī, coāctum**

Complete, I = **cōnficiō, -ere, cōnfēcī, cōnfectum**

Concerning = **dē** + abl.

Conduct, I = **gerō, -ere, gessī, gestum**

Conquer, I = **vincō, -ere, vīcī, victum**

Consul = **cōnsul, cōnsulis**, m.

Country = **patria, -ae**, f.

Country house = **vīlla, -ae**, f.

Countryside = **rūs, rūris**, n.

Courage = **virtūs, virtūtis**, f.

Cruel = **crūdēlis, -e**

Cruelly (adverb) = **crūdēliter**

Custom = **mōs, mōris**, m.

Danger = **perīculum, -ī**, n.

Dare, I = **audeō, audēre, ausus sum**

Daughter = **fīlia, -ae**, f. (dat. and abl. pl. = **fīliābus**)

Dawn (i.e. the first hour) = **prīma hōra, -ae**, f.; (i.e. first light) = **prīma lūx, lūcis**, f.

Day = diēs, diēī, m. (f. if an *appointed* day)

Dead = mortuus, -a, -um

Dear = cārus, -a, -um

Death = mors, mortis, f.

Decide, I = cōnstituō, -ere, cōnstituī, cōnstitūtum

Deep = altus, -a, -um

Defeat, I = vincō, vincere, vīcī, victum; superō, -āre, āvi, -ātum

Defend, I = dēfendō, -ere, dēfendī, dēfēnsum

Delay, I = moror, morārī, morātus sum

Delight, I = dēlectō, -āre, -āvī, -ātum

Depart, I = discēdō, -ere, discessī, discessum

Desire, I = cupiō, -ere, cupīvī, cupītum

Despair, I = dēspērō, -āre, -āvī, -ātum

Destroy, I = dēleō, dēlēre, dēlēvī, dēlētum

Die, I = morior, morī, mortuus sum; pereō, -īre, periī, peritum (*goes like* eō)

Difficult = difficilis, -e

Dine, I = cēnō, -āre, -āvī, -ātum

Dinner = cēna, -ae, f.

Do, I = faciō, -ere, fēcī, factum; agō, agere, ēgī, āctum

Dog = canis, canis, c.

Down from = dē + abl.

Drag, I = trahō, -ere, traxī, tractum

Dream (noun) = somnium, -iī, n.

Drink, I = bibō, -ere, bibī

Drive, I = pellō, -ere, pepulī, pulsum

Easily (adverb) = facile

Easy = facilis, -e

Eight = octŏ

Eighteen = duodēvīgintī

Eleven = ūndecim

Empire = imperium, -iī, n.

Encourage, I = hortor, -ārī, hortātus sum

End = fīnis, -is, m.

Enemy (public enemy, enemy of the state) = hostis, hostis, m. (usually used in plural)

Enemy (personal) = inimīcus, -ī, m.

Enough = satis

Enter = intrō, -āre, -āvī, -ātum

Escape, I = effugiō, -ere, effūgī

Even = etiam

Every = omnis, -e

Every day = cōtīdiē

Eye = oculus, -ī, m.

Faithful = fidēlis, -e

Faithfully (adverb) = fidēliter

Fall, I = cadō, -ere, cecidī, cāsum

Fame = fāma, -ae, f.

Famous = clārus, -a, -um

Farmer = agricola, -ae, m.

Father = pater, patris, m.

Fatherland = patria, -ae, f.

Fear, I = timeō, -ēre, -uī; vereor, -ērī, veritus sum

Few = paucī, -ae, -a

Field = ager, agrī, m.

Fifteen = quīndecim

Fight (noun) = pugna, -ae, f.

Fight, I = pugnō, -āre, -āvī, -ātum (intrans.; *use* cum +abl.)

Finally = postrēmō

Find, I = inveniō, -īre, invēnī, inventum

Fire (i.e. flames) = ignis, ignis, m.

Fire, a (i.e. a conflagration) = incendium, -iī, n.

First, at = prīmō / prīmum

Five = quīnque

Flee, I = fugiō, -ere, fūgī

Fleet = classis, classis, f.

Flight = fuga, -ae, f.

Flower = flōs, flōris, m.

Follow, I = sequor, sequī, secūtus sum

Food = cibus, -ī, m.

Foot = pēs, pedis, m.

Foot-soldier = pedes, peditis, m.

For = nam; enim (2nd word in clause)

For a long time = **diū**
Force, I = **cōgō, cōgere, coēgī, coāctum**
Forces = **cōpiae, -ārum**, f. pl.
Fortunate = **fēlīx, fēlīcis**
Fortunately (adverb) = **fēlīciter**
Fortune = **fōrtūna, -ae**, f.
Forum = **forum, -ī**, n.
Fountain = **fōns, fontis**, m.
Four = **quattuor**
Fourteen = **quattuordecim**
Free (adjective) = **līber, -era, -erum**
Free, I = **līberō, -āre, -āvī, -ātum**
Friend = **amīcus, -ī**, m.
From = **ā, ab** + abl.
From here, hence = **hinc**
From there, thence = **illinc**
Garden = **hortus, -ī**, m.
Gate = **porta, -ae**, f.
Gaul (the country) = **Gallia, -ae**, f.
Gaul (the person) = **Gallus, -ī**, m.
General = **imperātor, -ōris**, m.
Gift = **dōnum, -ī**, n.
Girl = **puella, -ae**, f.
Give back, I = **reddō, reddere, reddidī, redditum**
Give, I = **dō, dăre, dedī, dătum**
Glory = **fāma, -ae**, f.
Go back, I = **redeō, redīre, rediī, reditum** (*goes like* **eō**); **regredior, regredī, regressus sum**
Go down, I = **dēscendō, -ere, dēscendī, dēscēnsum**
Go forward, I = **prōgredior, prōgredī, prōgressus sum**
Go in, I = **intrō, -āre, -āvī, -ātum; ineō, -īre, iniī, initum** (*goes like* **eō**); **ingredior, ingredī, ingressus sum**
Go out, I = **exeō, exīre, exiī, exitum** (*goes like* **eō**); **ēgredior, ēgredī, ēgressus sum**
Go, I = **eō, īre, iī** (*or* **īvī**), **itum** (irreg.)
God = **deus, deī**, m. (irreg.)
Goddess = **dea, -ae**, f. (dat. and abl. pl. = **deābus**)

Gold = **aurum, -ī**, n.
Good = **bonus, -a, -um**
Grass = **herba, -ae**, f.
Great = **magnus, -a, -um**
Greatly (adverb) = **magnopere**
Greece = **Graecia, -ae**, f.
Greet, I = **salūtō, -āre, -āvī, -ātum**
Grief = **dolor, dolōris**, m.
Guard (noun) = **custōs, custōdis**, c.
Hall = **ātrium, ātriī**, n.
Hand = **manus, -ūs**, f.
Hand over, I = **trādō, -ere, trādidī, trāditum**
Happy = **laetus, -a, -um;** (= fortunate) **fēlīx, fēlīcis**
Harbour = **portus, -ūs**, m.
Hard = **dūrus, -a, -um**
Have, I = **habeō, -ēre, -uī, -itum**
Head = **caput, -itis**, n.
Hear, I = **audiō, -īre, -īvī, -ītum**
Heavy = **gravis, -e**
Hello = **salvē, salvēte**
Help = **auxilium, -iī**, n.
Help, I = **iuvō, iuvāre, iūvī, iūtum; adiuvō, -āre, adiūvī, adiūtum**
Her (own) = **suus, sua, suum**
Here = **hīc**
Hide, I = **cēlō, -āre, -āvī, -ātum**
High = **altus, -a, -um**
Hill = **collis, collis**, m.
His (own) = **suus, sua, suum**
Hold, I = **teneō, -ēre, tenuī, tentum**
Home = **domus, -ūs**, f. (irreg.); homewards = **domum**
Horn = **cornū, -ūs**, n.
Horse = **equus, equī**, m.
Horseman = **eques, equitis**, m.
Hour = **hōra, -ae**, f.
House = **domus, -ūs**, f. (irreg.)
How many? = **quot?**
How? = **quōmodŏ?**
However = **autem; tamen** (neither written as first word in clause)
Huge = **ingēns, ingentis**
Hundred, one = **centum**

Hurry, I = contendō, contendere, contendī, contentum

Hurry, I = festīnō, -āre, -āvī, -ātum

I = egŏ

If = sī

Immediately = statim

In = in + abl.

In vain = frūstrā

Infantry = peditēs, peditum, m. pl.

Inhabitant = incola, -ae, c.

Inn = taberna, -ae, f.

Into = in + acc.

Island = īnsula, -ae, f.

Italy = Ītalia, -ae, f.

Its (own) = suus, sua, suum

Journey = iter, itineris, n.

Joy = gaudium, gaudiī, n.

Judge = iūdex, iūdicis, c.

Jupiter = Iuppiter, Iovis, m.

Kill, I = necō, -āre, -āvī, -ātum; interficiō, -ere, interfēcī, interfectum; occīdō, -ere, occīdī, occīsum

King = rēx, rēgis, m.

Knee = genū, genūs, n.

Know, I = sciō, scīre, scīvī, scītum

Know, I do not = nesciō, -īre, -īvī, -ītum

Land = terra, -ae, f.

Laugh, I = rīdeō, -ēre, rīsī, rīsum

Law = lēx, lēgis, f.

Lead back, I = redūcō, -ere, redūxī, reductum

Lead, I = dūcō, -ere, dūxī, ductum

Leader = dux, ducis, c.

Learn (find out), I = cognōscō, -ere, cognōvī, cognitum

Learn, I = discō, -ere, didicī

Leave, I = relinquō, -ere, relīquī, relictum

Left = sinister, -tra, -trum

Legion = legiō, -ōnis, f.

Letter = epistola (*or* epistula), -ae, f.

Lie (down), I = iaceō, -ēre, iacuī, iacitum

Life = vīta, -ae, f.

Light = lūx, lūcis, f.

Like, I = amō, -āre, -āvī, -ātum

Lion = leō, leōnis, m.

Listen to, I = audiō, -īre, -īvī, -ītum

Live (inhabit), I = habitō, -āre, -āvī, -ātum

Long = longus, -a, -um

Long time, for a = diū

Longer (of time) = diūtius

Look at, I = spectō, -āre, -āvī, -ātum

Look! = ecce

Lord = dominus, -ī, m.

Love, I = amō, -āre, -āvī, -ātum

Make, I = faciō, -ere, fēcī, factum

Man (as opposed to woman) = vir, virī, m. (irreg.); (person) = homŏ, hominis, c.

Manage, I = gerō, -ere, gessī, gestum

Many = *see* Much

March, I = contendō, contendere, contendī, contentum

Marriage = mātrimōnium, -iī, n.

Master, schoolmaster = magister, magistrī, m.;

Master, lord = dominus, -ī, m.

Meanwhile = intereā

Message = nūntius, nūntiī, m.

Messenger = nūntius, nūntiī, m.

Middle = medius, -a, -um

Mind = animus, -ī, m.

Missile = tēlum, -ī, n.

Money = pecūnia, -ae, f.

Moon = lūna, -ae, f.

More (comparative of many) = plūs, plūris (neuter singular noun + genitive; *or* plural adjective)

More (adverb) = plūs

Moreover = autem (not first word in clause)

Most (superlative of many) = plūrimus, -a, -um

Mother = māter, mātris, f.

Mountain = mōns, montis, m.

Move (set in motion), I = **moveō, -ēre, mōvī, mōtum**

Much = **multus, -a, -um**

My = **meus, -a, -um**

Name = **nōmen, nōminis**, n.

Near = **prope** + acc.

Neither…nor = **nec…nec; neque…neque**

Never = **numquam**

New = **novus, -a, -um**

Night = **nox, noctis**, f.; (by night = **noctū**)

Nine = **novem**

Nineteen = **ūndēvīgintī**

No one = **nēmō, (nēminem, nūllīus, nēminī, nūllō)** c.

Nor = **nec; neque**

Not = **nōn**

Not know, I do = **nesciō, -īre, -īvī, -ītum**

Not only…but also = **nōn sōlum…sed etiam**

Nothing = **nihil**

Now = **iam; nunc**

Obey, I = **pāreō, -ēre, -uī, -itum** (+ dat.)

Often = **saepe**

Old (e.g. *x* years old) **annōs nātus, -a, -um**

Old man = **senex, senis**, m.

On = **in** + abl.

On account of = **propter** + acc.

On behalf of = **prō** + abl.

Once, once upon a time = **ōlim**

One = **ūnus, -a, -um** (gen. sing. = **ūnīus**, dat. sing. = **ūnī**)

Only, one only = **ūnus, -a, -um** (see above)

On to = **in** + acc.

Open, I = **aperiō, -īre, aperuī, apertum**

Order, I = **iubeō, -ēre, iussī, iussum**

Other = **alius, alia, aliud**

Other (of two) = **alter, altera, alterum**

Others, the rest = **cēterī, -ae, -a**

Other's, belonging to another = **aliēnus, -a, -um**

Ought, I = **dēbeō, -ēre, -uī, -itum**

Our = **noster, nostra, nostrum**

Out of = **ē / ex** + abl.

Outside = **extrā** + acc.

Over = **super** + acc.

Overcome, I = **superō, -āre, -āvī, -ātum**

Owe, I = **dēbeō, -ēre, -uī, -itum**

Pain = **dolor, dolōris**, m.

Pain, I feel = **doleō, -ēre, doluī, dolitum**

Parent = **parēns, parentis**, c.

Part = **pars, partis**, f.

Peace = **pāx, pācis**, f.

People (population) = **populus, -ī**, m.; (race, tribe) = **gēns, gentis**, f.

Perhaps = **fortasse**

Perish, I = **pereō, -īre, periī, peritum** (*goes like* **eō**)

Person = **homŏ, hominis**, c.

Persuade, I = **persuādeō, -ēre, persuāsī, persuāsum** (+ dat.)

Pitch camp, I = **castra pōnō**

Place (noun) = **locus, -ī**, m. (plural = **loca, -ōrum**, n. pl., when this refers to a region as opposed to single places)

Place, I = **pōnō, -ere, posuī, positum**

Plain = **campus, -ī**, m.

Plan = **cōnsilium, -iī**, n.

Plan, I adopt a = **cōnsilium capiō**

Play, I = **lūdō, -ere, lūsī, lūsum**

Pleasant = **dulcis, -e**

Poem = **carmen, carminis**, n.

Poet = **poēta, -ae**, m.

Praise, I = **laudō, -āre, -āvī, -ātum**

Pray, I = **ōrō, -āre, -āvī, -ātum**

Prepare, I = **parō, -āre, -āvī, -ātum**

Present, I am = **adsum, adesse, adfuī** (irreg.)

Price = **pretium, -iī**, n.

Prisoner = **captīvus, -ī**, m.

Promise, I = **prōmittō, -ere, prōmīsī, prōmissum**

Proud = **superbus, -a, -um**

Punish, I = **pūniō, -īre, -īvī, -ītum**

Queen = **rēgīna, -ae**, f.
Quick = **celer, celeris, celere**
Quickly (adverb) = **celeriter**
Read, I = **legō, -ere, lēgī, lēctum**
Rejoice, I = **gaudeō, gaudēre,
gāvīsus sum**
Remain, I = **maneō, -ēre, mānsī,
mānsum**
Reply, I = **respondeō, -ēre, respondī,
respōnsum**
Report, I = **nūntiō, -āre, -āvī, -ātum**
Return (come back), I = **reveniō, -īre,
revēnī, reventum**;
(give back), I = **reddō, reddere,
reddidī, redditum**;
(go back), I = **redeō, redīre, rediī,
reditum** (*goes like* **eō**); **regredior,
regredī, regressus sum**
Reward = **praemium, -iī**, n.
Right (as opposed to "left") = **dexter,
dextra, dextrum**
(as opposed to "wrong") = **rēctus,
-a, -um**
Rise, I = **surgō, -ere, surrēxī,
surrēctum**
River = **flūmen, flūminis**, n.
River-bank = **rīpa, -ae**, f.
Road = **via, -ae**, f.
Rock = **saxum, -ī**, n.
Roman (adjective) = **Rōmānus, -a, -um**
Roman (noun) = **Rōmānus, -ī**, m.
Rome = **Rōma, -ae**, f.
Rule, I = **regō, -ere, rēxī, rēctum**
Run, I = **currō, -ere, cucurrī, cursum**
Rush, I = **ruō, ruere, ruī, rutum**
Sacred = **sacer, sacra, sacrum**
Sad = **trīstis, trīste**
Sad, I am = **doleō, -ēre, doluī, dolitum**
Safe = **tūtus, -a, -um**
Sail, I = **nāvigō, -āre, -āvī, -ātum**
Sailor = **nauta, -ae**, m.
Same = **īdem, eadem, idem**
Savage = **saevus, -a, -um**
Save, I = **servō, -āre, -āvī, -ātum**
Say, I = **dīcō, dīcere, dīxī, dictum**

Say(s), he/she/they (quoting direct
speech) = **inquit/inquiunt**
School = **lūdus, -ī**, m.
Sea = **mare, maris**, n.
See, I = **videō, -ēre, vīdī, vīsum**
Seek, I = **petō, -ere, petīvī, petītum**;
quaerō, -ere, quaesīvī, quaesītum
Seem, I = **videor, vidērī, vīsus sum**
Seize, I = **occupō, -āre, -āvī, -ātum**
Self (intensive) = **ipse, ipsa, ipsum**
Self (reflexive) = **sē**
Send, I = **mittō, -ere, mīsī, missum**
Serious = **gravis, -e**
Set out, I = **proficīscor, proficīscī,
profectus sum**
Seven = **septem**
Seventeen = **septendecim**
Share, I = **partior, -īrī, partītus sum**
Shield = **scūtum, -ī**, n.
Ship = **nāvis, nāvis**, f.
Shop = **taberna, -ae**, f.
Shore = **ōra, -ae**, f.
Short = **brevis, breve**
Shout (noun) = **clāmor, -ōris**, m.
Shout, I = **clāmō, -āre, -āvī, -ātum**
Show, I = **ostendō, -ere, ostendī,
ostēnsum / ostentum**
Sign, signal = **signum, -ī**, n.
Silver = **argentum, -ī**, n.
Sing, I = **cantō, -āre, -āvī, -ātum**
Sister = **soror, -ōris**, f.
Sit, I = **sedeō, sedēre, sēdī, sessum**
Six = **sex**
Sixteen = **sēdecim**
Skill = **ars, artis**, f.
Sky = **caelum, -ī**, n.
Slave = **servus, -ī**, m.
Sleep (noun) = **somnus, -ī**, m.
Sleep, I = **dormiō, -īre, -īvī, -ītum**
Slowly (adverb) = **lentē**
Small = **parvus, -a, -um**
Smaller = **minor, minus**
Smallest = **minimus, -a, -um**
Smile, I = **rīdeō, -ēre, rīsī, rīsum**
So great = **tantus, -a, -um**

Soldier = **mīles, mīlitis**, c.

Son = **fīlius, fīliī** (or **fīlī**), m. (irreg.)

Song = **carmen, carminis**, n.

Soon = **mox**

Speak, I = **loquor, loquī, locūtus sum**

Spear = **hasta, -ae**, f.; **tēlum, -ī**, n.

Speech = **ōrātiō, -ōnis**, f.

Spirit = **animus, -ī**, m.

Stand, I = **stō, stāre, stetī, stătum**

Step = **gradus, gradūs**, m.

Storm = **tempestās, -ātis**, f.

Story = **fābula, -ae**, f.

Street = **via, -ae**, f.

Strong = **fortis, -e**; **valēns, -entis**; **validus, -a, -um**

Stupid = **stultus, -a, -um**

Such = **tālis, -e**

Suddenly = **subitō**

Summer = **aestās, -ātis**, f.

Sun = **sōl, sōlis**, m.

Swift = **celer, celeris, celere**

Sword = **gladius, gladiī**, m.

Table = **mēnsa, mēnsae**, f.

Take (seize), I = **capiō, -ere, cēpī, captum**

Task = **labor, labōris**, m.

Teach, I = **doceō, -ēre, docuī, doctum**

Tear = **lacrima, -ae**, f.

Tell (e.g. a story), I = **nārrō, -āre, -āvī, -ātum**

Temple = **templum, -ī**, n.

Ten = **decem**

Tender = **tener, -era, -erum**

Terrify, I = **terreō, -ēre, -uī, -itum**

Territory = **fīnēs, -ium**, m. pl.

Than = **quam**

Thanks, I give = **grātiās agō**

That (over there, yonder) = **ille, illa, illud**

That (near me) = **is, ea, id**

Theatre = **theātrum, -ī**, n.

Their (own) = **suus, sua, suum**

Then = **inde; tum; deinde; tunc**

There = **ibĭ**

There, in that place = **illīc**

There, thither, to there = **eō**

Therefore = **itaque; igitur** (not first word in clause); **ergŏ**

These: *see* this

Thing, matter = **rēs, reī**, f.

Think, I = **putō, -āre, -āvī, -ātum**

Thirteen = **tredecim**

This = **hic, haec, hoc**

Those: *see* that

Thousand = **mīlle**

Three = **trēs**

Through = **per** + acc.

Throw, I = **iaciō, -ere, iēcī, iactum**

Thus = **ita; sīc**

Time = **tempus, -ŏris**, n.

Tired = **fessus, -a, -um**

To, towards = **ad** + acc.

To here, hither = **hūc**

To there, thither = **illūc**

Today = **hodiē**

Together with = **cum** + abl.

Tomorrow = **crās**

Top of, topmost = **summus, -a, -um**

Touch, I = **tangō, tangere, tetigī, tāctum**

Towards = **ad** + acc.

Town = **oppidum, -ī**, n.

Treachery = **perfidia, -ae**, f.

Tree = **arbor, -ŏris**, f.

Troy = **Troia, -ae**, f.

Trust, I = **crēdō, -ere, crēdidī, crēditum** + dat.

Try, I = **cōnor, cōnārī, cōnātus sum**

Turn, I = **vertō, -ere, vertī, versum**

Twelve = **duodecim**

Twenty = **vīgintī**

Two = **duŏ**

Under = **sub** + abl.

Understand, I = **intellegō, -ere, intellēxī, intellēctum**

Urge, I = **hortor, -ārī, -ātus sum**

Use, I = **ūtor, ūtī, ūsus sum** (+ abl.)

Used to, I: *use* imperfect tense of verb (e.g. amābam = I *used to* love)

Victory = **victōria, -ae**, f.

Victory, I win a = **victōriam pariō**
Voice = **vōx, vōcis**, f.
Wage, I = **gerō, -ere, gessī, gestum**
Wait for, I = **exspectō, -āre, -āvī, -ātum**
Walk, I = **ambulō, -āre, -āvī, -ātum**
Wall = **mūrus, -ī**, m.
Wander, I = **errō, -āre, -āvī, -ātum**
Want, I = **cupiō, -ere, -īvī, -ītum**
War = **bellum, -ī**, n.
Warn, I = **moneō, -ēre, -uī, -itum**
Watch, I = **spectō, -āre, -āvī, -ātum**
Water = **aqua, -ae**, f.
Wave = **unda, -ae**, f.
Way (method) = **modus, -ī**, m.
Way (street) = **via, -ae**, f.
We = **nōs**
Weapons = **arma, -ōrum**, n. pl.
Wear, I = **gerō, -ere, gessī, gestum**
Weather = **tempestās, -ātis**, f.
Weep, I = **fleō, flēre, flēvī, flētum**
Well (adverb) = **bene**
Well-known = **nōtus, -a, -um**
What? = **quid?**
When (conjunction) = **ubǐ**
When? (adverb) = **quandǒ?**
Where (conjunction) = **ubǐ**
Where? (adverb) = **ubǐ ?**
While = **dum**
Who, which = **quī, quae, quod**
Who? = **quis?**
Whole = **tōtus, -a, -um** (*goes like* **ūnus**)
Why? = **cūr?**
Wife = **uxor, -ōris**, f.
Wind = **ventus, -ī**, m.

Wing (of an army) = **cornū, -us**, n.
Wisdom = **sapientia, -ae**, f.
Wise = **sapiēns, sapientis**
Wisely (adverb) = **sapienter**
With (i.e. together with) = **cum** + abl.
Within = **intrā** + acc.
Without = **sine** + abl.
Woman = **fēmina, -ae**, f.; **mulier, mulieris**, f.
Wonder at, I = **mīror, mīrārī, mīrātus sum**
Wood, forest = **silva, -ae**, f.
Word = **verbum, -ī**, n.
Work (noun) = **opus, operis**, n.; **labor, labōris**, m.
Work, I = **labōrō, -āre, -āvī, -ātum**
Worse = **peior, -us**
Worst = **pessimus, -a, -um**
Worthy (of) = **dignus, -a, -um** + abl.
Wound (noun) = **vulnus, vulneris**, n.
Wound, I = **vulnerō, -āre, -āvī, -ātum**
Wretched = **miser, -era, -erum**
Write, I = **scrībō, -ere, scrīpsī, scrīptum**
Year = **annus, -ī**, m.
Yesterday = **herī**
You (plural) = **vōs**
You (singular) = **tū**
Young man, young person = **iuvenis, iuvenis**, c.
Your (belonging to you (plural)) = **vester, vestra, vestrum**
Your (belonging to you (singular)) = **tuus, -a, -um**